Praise for *The Happiness Equation*

"I'm blown away by *The Happiness Equation*. Neil's nine secrets will improve how you think, how you feel, and how you act! All in two hours. Read this book—it's the *best* twenty dollars you will ever spend!"

—KEN BLANCHARD,
coauthor of *The New One Minute Manager* and
Refire! Don't Retire

"When Neil Pasricha talks, leaders of all levels and backgrounds stop what they're doing . . . and listen."

—HOWARD BEHAR,
former president, Starbucks Coffee

"Dale Carnegie was last century. Stephen Covey was last decade. Neil Pasricha is what's now. *The Happiness Equation* is a two-hour ticket to changing your life!"

—SUSAN CAIN,
author of *Quiet* and cofounder, Quiet Revolution

"This book does one of the best jobs I have ever seen in explaining happiness! While everyone else implies that happiness is 'out there,' Neil points out that it is really 'in here'!"

—MARSHALL GOLDSMITH,
coauthor of *What Got You Here Won't Get You There*

"This lighthearted and compelling book presents commonsense suggestions for achieving happiness that will most definitely motivate new rituals and change habits in your life."

—STEVE REINEMUND,
former Chairman and CEO, PepsiCo, and former Dean,
Wake Forest University School of Business

"Neil Pasricha is a life coach for the next generation! In *The Happiness Equation*, he makes happiness attainable by using scientifically proven habits that require low time investment and reap massive rewards!"

—SHAWN ACHOR,
author of *The Happiness Advantage*

"With simple effortlessness, Neil renders complex ideas easily memorable and everyday practical. Disarmingly written, memorably fun, and unstoppingly useful. Reading it made me immediately want to give it to everyone I know!"

—COL. CHRIS HADFIELD,
former Commander of the International Space Station
and author of *The Astronaut's Guide to Life on Earth*

"Neil's new book *The Happiness Equation* is a treat, an enticing journey that helped me identify and overcome the obstacles we all set on our path to happiness. His playful writing comes across as friendly advice without the painful refrain of artificial rules that typically characterize so-called self-help advice."

"*The Happiness Equation* has great information that will lead to tremendous changes in both your professional and personal life!"

"*The Happiness Equation* shows you how to live life on your own terms. A dazzling and highly useful action book I'll be giving to everyone I know!"

"How is it possible for subtle, nonjudgmental lessons to hit you on the head like the proverbial ton of bricks? I'm not sure how he did it, but Neil Pasricha is *the* modern-day master of what it means to live intentionally. I loved this book!"

"Neil has a way of creating a moment in time and shares many unique lessons on how you can live a happier more purposeful life. His ability to connect with his readers is not only impactful but transformational. In *The Happiness Equation* he offers intimate lessons on how you can live a truly rich life in a way that is tangible and fun. Happiness and freedom are free and attainable—and this book helps light the path!"

—BRUE POON TIP,
Founder and CEO, G Adventures, the largest adventure travel company in the world, and author of *Looptail*

"Ready for world-class happiness? This powerful book is your mighty guide."

—ROBIN SHARMA,
author of *The Leader Who Had No Title*

"The *awesome* Neil Pasricha turns his keen powers of observation and his extensive experience in leadership building to the subject of happiness. Clear, practical, and thought-provoking, *The Happiness Equation* reveals how all of us can live happier lives."

—GRETCHEN RUBIN,
author of *The Happiness Project*

"With self-effacing humor and disarming honesty, Neil shares insights gained from his own personal experiences, in a book you simply can't put down. Whether you relate instantaneously to his stories or engage from a distance, his simple rules stick with you. They are clear beacons guiding the way to a more conscious and fulfilled life."

—AMEE CHANDE,
Managing Director, Alibaba UK, and Board Member, World Association of Girl Guides and Girl Scouts

"Neil joined the Audi Executive Team across the United States and his happiness lessons were the highlight of the show, engaging dealer associates, and invigorating the audience. He is always on point, thought-provoking, and receives near-perfect ratings. Listen to him!"

—PETER DONNELLAN,
Director, After Sales, Audi of America

"*The Four-Hour Work Week* meets *The Happiness Project* in *The Happiness Equation*—an incredible book that gave me time-saving tips in the first few minutes and a genuinely happier life by the end. Neil is the master of happiness. Buy this book!"

—BILL MARSHALL,
cofounder, Toronto International Film Festival

"The interactions, trust, healing, laughter, camaraderie, sadness, and vulnerabilities that come with taking care of patients are gifts to be enjoyed and appreciated. Sadly, the prism where we can see these qualities becomes rapidly clouded. There is a real role for Neil's work within health care. The more penetration his philosophies have, the more satisfaction, quality, and longevity we'll see."

—DR. MARK SHAPIRO,
Sharp HealthCare

"Neil Pasricha has done it again! With his best-seller *The Book of Awesome* he shared the observation of awesome. And now with *The Happiness Equation* he shifts to the application of awesome. Prepare yourself before reading. Nobody has hacked happiness like this before!"

—FRANK WARREN,
author of *PostSecret*

"Being happy is the biggest challenge in life. *The Happiness Equation* is full of reminders of ways we know we can increase our happiness and also supplies wholly new approaches based on scientific research and common sense. It feels like Neil is talking to you. The secrets are simple, and Neil's explanations and enthusiasm make you want to start practicing all of them immediately."

—BARBARA ANN KIPFER,
author of *14,000 Things to Be Happy About*

"Neil Pasricha takes us on a journey of incredible self-discovery. Easy to read + practical solutions = the best happiness book ever written."

—JIM THOMPSON,
COO, Walmart China

"Neil Pasricha has created *the* Handbook for Life. Every day we are faced with a barrage of inputs that deflect us from being present with the things that really matter. The things that make us happy. Page by page, Neil weaves beautiful anecdotes into simple secrets for everyday life. The result: we are given the tools to sort perspectives and information in a way that allows us to see the goodness that the real world holds for us. Bravo, and thank you."

—DAVID HAY,
former Managing Director, Merrill Lynch

"You know that wise friend you have? The one you call when you need hope, perspective, and someone to give you permission to do and think the things you know are best for you? Reading this book is like having wine with that friend."

—DREW DUDLEY,
CEO, Nuance Leadership

"If you want to live your dreams now—not in five, ten or twenty years—then buy *The Happiness Equation* today. It is impossible to read this book without making changes that lead to living a more fulfilling life. Even if you're in your eighties like me!"

—ROBERT WRIGHT,
former Chairman, Teck Resources

"Neil has masterfully distilled happiness. Both beautiful and pragmatic, Neil's treatise elicits tears of acknowledgment and awakens the dormant reverie of a happier future."

—JORDAN AXANI,
CEO, Triplust

"I've spent my life on the math of relationships, but this book entails the science of something I never covered at OkCupid: a person's relationship with himself. It's an excellent guide to making that relationship the strongest and happiest it can be."

—CHRISTIAN RUDDER,
cofounder, OKCupid, and author of *Dataclysm*

"Be happy first. These three words are so counterintuitive that most of us don't know what to do with them. Neil does."

—SETH GODIN,
author of *What to Do When It's Your Turn*

"Want to get happy? Steal everything you can from this book."

—AUSTIN KLEON,
author of *Steal Like an Artist*

3 Ways to
Get the Most out of This Book

3. **Agree to disagree.** You will not agree with all nine secrets the first time you read them. That's okay. Expect to disagree. But remember you have the power to slowly let new ideas into your brain whenever you like. A hundred years before neuroplasticity became a buzzword, American philosopher William James said, "Plasticity, in the wide sense of the word, means the possession of a structure weak enough to yield to an influence but strong enough not to yield all at once."

2. **Change your scenery.** Reading this book cover to cover in one night is fine. But if you change your scenery, you'll get more out of it. A chapter in the buzzing airport, a chapter at the beach, a chapter in bed before flicking off your lamp. Our brains are stimulated by different air, smells, and sounds. Everywhere you read the book you'll get something different from it and you'll more easily recall the lessons. Carry this book as you're moving.

1. **Create a seven-day challenge.** Any time you read an idea in this book that you want to try, give yourself a seven-day challenge. Write down every day in your calendar for seven days "Do X" and then try to do it. If you can do it for seven days, you just proved you could do it for seven days. Then you can do it for another seven days. Then it becomes a habit. Aristotle says, "We are what we repeatedly do. Excellence, then, is not an act, but a habit."

The
Happiness
Equation

Want Nothing + Do Anything
= Have Everything

Neil Pasricha

G. P. PUTNAM'S SONS
New York

PUTNAM

G. P. PUTNAM'S SONS
Publishers Since 1838
An imprint of Penguin Random House LLC
375 Hudson Street
New York, New York 10014

Library of Congress Cataloging-in-Publication Data
Pasricha, Neil.
The happiness equation : want nothing + do anything = have everything / Neil Pasricha.
p.   cm.
ISBN 978-0-399-16947-2 (hardback)
1. Happiness.   2. Conduct of life   3. Success.   I. Title.
BJ1481.P58   2016   2015015845
158—dc23

International edition ISBN 978-0-399-57695-9

Printed in the United States of America
1 3 5 7 9 10 8 6 4 2

BOOK DESIGN BY TANYA MAIBORODA

Some names and details have been changed in the stories in this book.

To my baby,
I wanted you to have this in case I didn't get a chance to tell you,
Love, Dad

Contents

Want Nothing

Secret #1
The First Thing You Must Do Before You Can Be Happy

Secret #2
Do This and Criticism Can't Touch You

Secret #3
The Three Words That Will Save You on Your Very Worst Days

Do Anything

Secret #4
The Dream We All Have That Is Completely Wrong

Secret #5
How to Make More Money Than a Harvard MBA

Secret #6
The Secret to Never Being Too Busy Again

Have Everything

Secret #7
....
How to Turn Your Biggest Fear into Your Biggest Success

Secret #8
The Simple Way to Master Your Most Important Relationship

Secret #9
The Single Best Piece of Advice You'll Ever Take

Author's Note

I have spent more than a decade developing leaders.

I have had incredible experiences speaking about leadership to hundreds of thousands of people around the world, eating dinner with royal families in the Middle East, sharing stages with Harvard deans, and consulting on leadership to organizations like Audi, Viacom, and GE. I have worked as Director of Leadership Development at Walmart, interviewed billionaires, and worked directly for two CEOs at the world's largest company.

But after years successfully helping people lead teams, lead businesses, and lead organizations, something slowly dawned on me.

Hardly anyone was happy.

Every conference lunch was filled with conversations about struggling to find balance, feeling too busy, and keeping up with others. So many leaders said they didn't have space in their lives, were stressed about time and money, and felt burdened with endless decisions and conflicting advice. Even the greatest leaders in the world—even billionaires, even Fortune 500 CEOs—were all plagued with dramatic crises on a daily basis. Fiery cauldrons of stress were bubbling in their heads and stomachs.

I also realized I wasn't happy myself.

I was searching for simple models to decide what to do, searching for structure to relieve stress, and searching for guidelines to steer me through tough decisions constantly bogging me down. I thought about all the times I felt guilty not getting work done, burned out after a crazy week, or struggling in messy mental states for days navigating tough choices.

Looking back, I can't believe how much time I wasted.

Being happier is the biggest challenge you face every single day at work. Same if you're a stay-at-home mom, studying through school, or traveling abroad. Teaching and training your brain to stay positively focused while navigating the bumps of life is something we're not taught at school. I mean, have you ever taken a course called "How to Be Happier"?

For the past few years, I have led workshops every summer with high school students who are brought together for the entire month of July for a world-class enrichment camp. These students have the highest grades in their schools, participate in the most clubs and teams, and are all destined for Ivy Leagues. They love the program because they get to meet and spend time with people like them. I do the workshops because I was lucky enough to attend when I was in high school.

What started organically, with no notes and no slides, has slowly evolved into a talk I give called "9 Secrets to a Happier Life." And at the end of my talk I open up to questions. I am always surprised by what is asked. The students don't have questions about getting better grades, getting into the best schools, or landing the highest-paid jobs. They know they can do all that. Everything they ask comes from a desire to be happier.

"How much money do I need to retire?" "What's the best way to handle criticism?" "How do I get more done with less stress?" "How do I find my true passion?" "How can I cure my anxiety?" "What's the best way to achieve more inside and outside work?" "What do I do when everyone gives me different advice?" "How can I become a more positive person?"

The sessions are illuminating because they show how some of

the smartest kids around don't care about developing brainpower or technical smarts. They want *contentment . . . freedom . . .* and *happiness*. They want to *want nothing . . . do anything . . .* and *have everything*.

They just want to live happier lives.

So don't you think every college, university, and library would be full of courses and advice on how we can become happier? On how we can make decisions that spur ourselves into positive action every day?

When I asked a hospitality CEO if he knew a book, model, or website that actually helped people navigate and simplify their most challenging decisions so they can live with contentment, freedom, and happiness, he said, "That book doesn't exist. It would be like asking every high-powered executive, successful person, and positive leader to distill all the personal mental models they've created over their lives into one book. Nobody has ever done it."

I know this is true because I've been searching for a practical book with real frameworks on leading myself to happiness for years. I wanted something beyond stories about generals, parables about penguins, and research studies with data pointing any which way. I wanted real, I wanted practical, I wanted clear. I wanted an action book that I could use every day.

This is that book.

Want
Nothing

Be content with what you have. Rejoice in the way
 things are.
When you realize there is nothing lacking, the
 whole world belongs to you.

—LAO TZU

True happiness is to enjoy the present, without
anxious dependence upon the future, not to amuse
ourselves with either hopes or fears but to rest satisfied with what we have, which is sufficient, for he
that is so wants nothing. The greatest blessings of
mankind are within us and within our reach. A
wise man is content with his lot, whatever it may
be, without wishing for what he has not.

—SENECA

You can't have everything. Where would you
put it?

—STEVEN WRIGHT

Secret #1

The First Thing

You Must Do

Before You Can

Be Happy

1

6 words that will forever change how you see happiness

L et's start off with some bad news.

The happiness model we're taught from a young age is actually completely backward.

We think we work hard in order to achieve big success and then we're happy.

We think the scribble goes like this:

GREAT WORK → BIG SUCCESS → BE HAPPY

Study hard! → Straight A's! → Be happy!

Interview lots! → Great job! → Be happy!

Work overtime! → Get promoted! → Be happy!

But it doesn't work like that in real life. That model is broken. We do great work, have a big success, but instead of being happy, we just set new goals. Now we study for the next job, the next degree, the next promotion. Why stop at a college degree when you can get a master's? Why stop at Director when you can be VP? Why stop at one house when you can have two? We never get to happiness. It keeps getting pushed further and further away.

What happens when we snap "Be happy" off the end of this

scribble and stick it on the beginning? Then these important six words look like this:

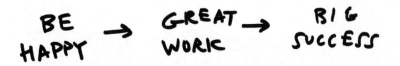

Now everything changes. *Everything* changes. If we start with being happy, then we feel great. We look great. We exercise. We connect. What happens? We end up doing great work because we *feel* great doing it. What does great work lead to? Big success. Massive feelings of accomplishment and the resulting degrees, promotions, and phone calls from your mom telling you she's proud of you.

Harvard Business Review reports that happy people are 31% more productive, have 37% higher sales, and are three times more creative than their counterparts.

So what's the *first* thing you must do before you can be happy?

Be happy.

Be happy *first*.

Being happy opens up your learning centers. Your brain will light up like Manhattan skyscrapers at dusk, sparkle like diamonds under jewelry store lights, glow like stars in the black sky above a farmer's field.

American philosopher William James says, "The greatest discovery of any generation is that a human being can alter his life by altering his attitude."

The Happiness Advantage author Shawn Achor says, "It's not necessarily the reality that shapes us but the lens through which your brain views the world that shapes your reality."

William Shakespeare says, "For there is nothing either good or bad, but thinking makes it so."

2

The single biggest reason it's so hard to be happy

Shakespeare says, "For there is nothing either good or bad, but thinking makes it so." But if it's just thinking, plain thinking, why can't we *think* ourselves into a good mood whenever we want? Seems like we should be able to just flip a mental switch.

But we all know it's not that easy. Sometimes our brains get focused on negative things. We can't stop! I do this all the time. And you want to know a secret? Everybody does. Every single person gets stuck focusing on the negative sometimes. I've spoken on stages with the best-known motivational speakers, Fortune 500 CEOs, and political leaders from around the world. Do you know what they're all doing backstage? Freaking out. Sweating. Thinking something might go wrong.

We all have negative self-talk. There is no such thing as an eternal optimist. There are people who feel optimistic, but those people have negative self-talk, too. And that's okay. The problem isn't that we have negative thoughts in our brain.

The problem is we think we shouldn't have negative thoughts.

But *why* do our brains focus on negative things? Once we understand this we can learn how much we can control and make conscious efforts to be happy using proven techniques.

This is one of the most important things I can share with you.

Why is it so hard to be happy?

Because life was mostly short, brutal, and highly competitive over the two hundred thousand years our species has existed on this planet. And our brains are trained for this short, brutal, and highly competitive world.

How short, brutal, and highly competitive was it?

Let's do a quick experiment.

Stop, close your eyes, and picture the last time you felt completely alone in the middle of nowhere.

Was it camping in the mountains when you walked away from the fire and stood on the jagged edge of a mirrory lake? Was it a misty waterfall you found on a field trip when your classmates disappeared and all you could hear was the wind rustling the leaves in the forest canopy? Was it jogging at sunrise on a sandy beach when you curled around the coastline and suddenly couldn't see anyone for miles in any direction?

Picture yourself back in that scene.

Now mentally erase from our planet all of the following:

• Toilets	• Cars	• Fridges
• Sinks	• Planes	• Freezers
• Showers	• Boats	• Farms
• Running water	• Books	• Stoves
• Computers	• Paper	• Microwaves
• Phones	• Pencils	• Shirts
• Internet	• Pens	• Sweaters
• Beds	• Hospitals	• Jackets
• Chairs	• Doctors	• Pants
• Roads	• Medicines	• Socks
• Bikes	• Tools	• Shoes
	• Grocery stores	• Underwear

You are now standing alone in the middle of the planet with none of those things. Take your phone out of your pocket and toss it away. Take your shoes and shirt off, too, because they don't exist. Take everything off. You are completely naked with nothing around. None of those things exist. And none of them will begin to exist before the end of your life!

Now close your eyes, picture yourself there, and remember that:

99% of our history was living in this world.

99% of our history was with a life span of thirty years.

99% of our history was with brains **constantly battling for survival.**

Life was short, brutal, and highly competitive, and we have the same brains now that we've had throughout our history.

Were we happy back then? The better question is: Did we have time to be happy?

David Cain, author of *This Will Never Happen Again*, describes this exact situation on his website Raptitude: Getting Better at Being Human:

> If one of our ancestors ever actually became happy with his possessions, with his social standing, or with what he had accomplished in life, he would suddenly be in a particular kind of danger. There was no cradle of civilization to depend on if something went wrong. So survival required us to make our own safety nets. Having enough could never feel like enough, or else we'd become complacent, leaving us vulnerable to predators, competitors, and bad luck. Lasting happiness was too risky.

This instinctive need for what we don't yet have creates in us a persistent state of dissatisfaction. Without it, our ancestors would always be only one failed hunting session away from starvation. This simple, ruthless script is programmed to drive survival at all costs. It works exceedingly well for this purpose, but it leaves us feeling stress and unpleasantness much of the time. Unhappiness is nature's way of keeping people on their toes. It's a crude system, but it has worked for thousands of years.

We have the same brains we've always had through this short, brutal, and highly competitive time in our history. Our brains didn't just suddenly change when we got printing presses, airplanes, and the Internet. How have our brains been programmed?

Year	→	"I need..."	→	"If I don't, I'll..."
180,000 BCE	→	Food and safety	→	Die
170,000 BCE	→	Food and safety	→	Die
160,000 BCE	→	Food and safety	→	Die
150,000 BCE	→	Food and safety	→	Die
140,000 BCE	→	Food and safety	→	Die
130,000 BCE	→	Food and safety	→	Die
120,000 BCE	→	Food and safety	→	Die
110,000 BCE	→	Food and safety	→	Die
100,000 BCE	→	Food and safety	→	Die
90,000 BCE	→	Food and safety	→	Die
80,000 BCE	→	Food and safety	→	Die
70,000 BCE	→	Food and safety	→	Die
60,000 BCE	→	Food and safety	→	Die
50,000 BCE	→	Food and safety	→	Die
40,000 BCE	→	Food and safety	→	Die
30,000 BCE	→	Food and safety	→	Die
20,000 BCE	→	Food and safety	→	Die
10,000 BCE	→	Food and safety	→	Die
1	→	Food and safety	→	Die
1000	→	Food and safety	→	Die
2000	→	Happiness	→	Die

What did this fear do? It drove our survival. We survived at all costs. We were paranoid. We were fighters. We were ruthless. We were brutal. We were murderous. And because of it . . . we got here. And because of it . . . we took over the planet. And because of it . . . we have everything in the world.

So this begs the question: Is that fear still programmed into our heads today?

3

The one thing your doctor, teacher, and Tom Hanks all have in common

Yes, that fear is still programmed into our heads.

It's everywhere, it's between our ears, it's in our brains.

Tom Hanks, one of the world's most successful actors, who earns millions with every movie and has scored two Academy Awards, said, "Some people go to bed at night thinking, 'That was a good day.' I am one of those who worries and asks, 'How did I screw up today?'"

Andy Grove is the longtime Intel executive who helped transform the company into a multibillion-dollar success. He was believed by many to have helped drive the growth phase of Silicon Valley, was named *Time*'s Man of the Year in 1997, and was idolized by Steve Jobs, according to Jobs's biography. How did he famously put it? "Only the paranoid survive."

Our brains still follow this paranoid model every day, and it is a recipe for unhappiness! Some call it Medical Student's Syndrome. That's a term Jerome K. Jerome first coined in his 1889 classic, *Three Men in a Boat*: "I remember going to the British Museum one day to read up the treatment for some slight ailment of which I had a touch—hay fever, I fancy it was. I got down the book, and read all I came to read; and then, in an unthinking moment, I idly turned the leaves, and began to indolently study diseases, generally. I forget which was the first distemper I plunged into—some fearful, devastating scourge, I know—and, before I had glanced half down the list of 'premonitory symptoms,' it was borne in upon me that I had fairly got it.

"I sat for a while, frozen with horror; and then, in the listlessness of despair, I again turned over the pages. I came to typhoid fever—read the symptoms—discovered that I had typhoid fever, must have had it for months without knowing it—wondered what else I had got; turned up St. Vitus's Dance—found, as I expected, that I had that, too—began to get interested in my case, and determined to sift it to the bottom, and so started alphabetically—read up ague, and learnt that I was sickening for it, and that the acute stage would commence in about another fortnight . . ."

It's not just medical students. We've all been there.

We scan the world for problems because that led to our survival. And our current design of the world only reinforces and grows these negative-lens feelings.

At your doctor's office when you get lab results, the doctor says, "Your blood sugar is fine, your cholesterol is fine, but your iron is low." What do you do? You talk about getting your iron up. Eat steak! No work is done improving your blood sugar or cholesterol. If cholesterol should be below 200mg/dL and you're at 195, great! If you're 205, that's a problem. Doctors get paid when we're sick. Shouldn't we pay them when we're healthy?

Retail store managers "manage by exception" by staring at morning reports, finding a number below average, and trying to bump it up. If that report says your traffic count is fine, basket size is fine, but checkout time is below average, what does the boss want? Faster checkouts. More cashiers! No work is done improving statistics that are already average.

In the classroom the teacher hands back test results and offers extra help to those below average. They have to pass! If not, the year is repeated, the system is drained, friends all move ahead. What happens for the below-average kids? Extra help at lunch. Tutoring sessions. Remedial tests. Why aren't students who get 100% offered any extra challenge?

It's no different in the workplace. We get job evaluations showing how well we're doing. What happens if you're below expectations? Performance improvement plan! Extra meetings with the boss! Shipped to training classes! What happens if you're doing well? Two percent raise. Pat on the back.

Rather than find good results and make them better, our brains do this:

1. Look for problem.
2. Find problem.
3. Improve problem.

That's what our brains have been trained to do for two hundred thousand years. But because we scan the world for problems, sometimes that's all we see. Here's how *New York Times*–bestselling author Kelly Oxford framed our Medical Student's Syndrome on Twitter: "WebMD is like a Choose Your Own Adventure book where the ending is always cancer."

So what do we do about it?

4

How much can we control?

Aristotle says, "Happiness depends upon ourselves."

Viktor Frankl says, "Everything can be taken from a man but one thing: the last of the human freedoms—to choose one's attitude in any given set of circumstances, to choose one's own way."

Walt Whitman writes, "Keep your face always toward the sunshine—and shadows will fall behind you."

I love what Artistotle, Viktor Frankl, and Walt Whitman say. But how do you get there?

Well, we now have scientific evidence of the importance of attitude and specific proven actions we can take to manage our attitude.

When my wife Leslie turned sixteen, her grandmother gave her a brass-framed quote for her birthday. She hung it on her bedroom wall. She looked at it in the mornings before school, and it is still hanging in her old bedroom today. I have stopped to read it several times, and I took a picture to show you.

Pay special attention to the second last sentence:

Attitude

"The longer I live, the more I realize the impact of attitude on life. Attitude, to me, is more important than facts. It is more important than the past, than education, than money, than circumstances than failures, than successes, than what other people think or say or do. It is more important than appearance, giftedness or skill. It will make or break a company.... a church.... a home.... a friendship. The remarkable thing is we have a choice every day regarding the attitude we will embrace for that day. We cannot change our past...we cannot change the fact that people will act in a certain way. We cannot change the inevitable. The only thing we can do is play on the one we have, and that is our attitude.... I am convinced that life is 10% what happens and 90% how I react to it. And so it is with you...We are in charge of our Attitudes."

Sam Walton

I know it says Sam Walton on the poster! But this is an artifact of the old days when email forwards and chain letters had misattributions that lasted for years. This quote was actually said by Charles Swindoll, a Texas preacher who broadcasts a show to more than two thousand radio stations.

Do you know what's amazing about this quote?

The second last sentence!

"I am convinced that life is 10% what happens and 90% how I react to it."

Well, new research published in *The How of Happiness* by University of California psychology professor Sonja Lyubomirsky tells us exactly how much of our happiness is based on our life circumstances.

And it is 10%!

10% of our happiness is what happens *to* us.

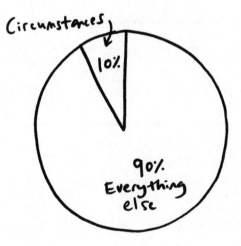

So 90% of our happiness isn't based on what's happening in the world! *It's based on how we see the world.* What's included in the 90%? Our genetic predisposition and our intentional activities. Yes, intentional activities. This is big. Those are *specific things* we can do to improve our happiness. And they alone have *four times the effect on our happiness* than anything happening in our life.

Let me put it another way:

If I knew everything about your life circumstances—your job, your health, your marital status, your income—I could predict only 10% of your happiness. That's it! The remaining amount is not determined by your external world but by the way your brain processes it.

5

7 ways to be happy right now

How do you be happy first?

For this chapter we look to the emerging field of positive psychology. What's that? It's not fluffy lollipop experiments. Professors of psychology Martin Seligman and Mihaly Csikszentmihalyi are called the fathers of positive psychology because of their passion for cold hard facts. As they put it themselves in *American Psychologist*:

"Psychology is not just a branch of medicine concerned with illness or health; it is much larger. It is about work, education, insight, love, growth, and play. And in this quest for what is best, positive psychology does not rely on wishful thinking, faith, self-deception, fads, or hand-waving; it tries to adapt what is best in the scientific method to the unique problems that human behavior presents to those who wish to understand it in all its complexity."

Positive psychology is a new and growing field.

I have sifted through hundreds of studies to find the **Big 7** ways to train your brain to be happy. Many of these studies have been discussed in journals, conference keynotes, and research reports, but I've brought them together for you here.

If you do any of these seven things for two straight weeks, you will feel happier.

So what are the Big 7?

THREE WALKS
THE 20-MINUTE REPLAY
RANDOM ACTS OF KINDNESS
A COMPLETE UNPLUG
HIT FLOW
2-MINUTE MEDITATIONS
FIVE GRATITUDES

Three Walks

Pennsylvania State researchers reported in the *Journal of Sport & Exercise Psychology* that the more physically active people are, the greater their general feelings of excitement and enthusiasm. Researcher Amanda Hyde reports, "We found that people who are more physically active have more pleasant-activated feelings than people who are less active, and we also found that people have more pleasant-activated feelings on days when they are more physically active than usual." It doesn't take much: Half an hour of brisk walking three times a week improves happiness. The American Psychosomatic Society published a study showing how Michael Babyak and a team of doctors found that three thirty-minute brisk walks or jogs even improve recovery from clinical depression. Yes, *clinical depression*. Results were stronger than studies using medication or studies using exercise and medication combined.

The 20-Minute Replay

Writing for twenty minutes about a positive experience dramatically improves happiness. Why? Because you actually re*live* the experience as you're writing it and then re*live* it every time you read it. Your brain sends you back. In a University of Texas study called "How Do I Love Thee? Let Me Count the Words," researchers Richard Slatcher and James Pennebaker had one member of a couple write about their relationship for twenty minutes three times a day. Compared to the test group, the couple was more likely to engage in intimate dialogue afterward and the relationship was more likely to last. What does the 20-Minute Replay do? It helps us remember things we like about people and experiences in our lives.

Random Acts of Kindness

Carrying out five random acts of kindness a week dramatically improves your happiness. We don't naturally think about paying for someone's coffee, mowing our neighbor's lawn, or writing a thank-you note to our apartment building security guard at Christmas. But Sonja Lyubomirsky, author of *The How of Happiness*, did a study asking Stanford students to perform five random acts of kindness over a week. Not surprisingly, they reported much higher happiness levels than the test group. Why? They felt good about themselves! People appreciated them. In his book *Flourish*, Professor Martin Seligman says that "we scientists have found that doing a kindness produces the single most reliable momentary increase in well-being of any exercise we have tested."

A Complete Unplug

"The richest, happiest and most productive lives are characterized by the ability to fully engage in the challenge at hand, but also to disengage periodically and seek renewal," say Jim Loehr and Tony Schwartz in *The Power of Full Engagement.* And a Kansas State University study found that complete downtime after work helps us recharge for the next day. Turning your phone off after dinner. Not using the Internet on vacation. There's a lot more to this, and we're going to chat about it in Secret #6. If you can't wait, flip to page 145.

Hit Flow

Get into a groove. Be in the zone. Find your flow. However you characterize it, when you're completely absorbed with what you're doing, it means you're being challenged and demonstrating skill at the same time. Mihaly Csikszentmihalyi describes this moment as "being completely involved in an activity for its own sake. The ego falls away. Time flies. Every action, movement, and thought follows inevitably from the previous one, like playing jazz. Your whole being is involved, and you're using your skills to the utmost." In his book *Flow: The Psychology of Optimal Experience,* he describes it using an image I've redrawn on the following page:

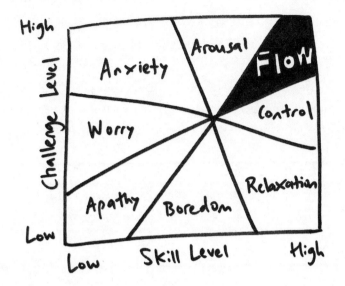

2-Minute Meditations

A research team from Massachusetts General Hospital looked at brain scans of people before and after they participated in a course on mindfulness meditation and published the results in *Psychiatry Research*. What happened? After the course, parts of the brain associated with compassion and self-awareness grew while parts associated with stress shrank. Studies report that meditation can "permanently rewire" your brain to raise levels of happiness.

Five Gratitudes

If you can be happy with simple things, then it will be simple to be happy. Find a book or a journal, or start a website, and write down three to five things you're grateful for from the past week. I wrote five a week on 1000awesomethings.com. Some people write in a notebook by their bedside. Back in 2003, researchers Robert Emmons and Michael McCullough asked groups of students to write down five gratitudes, five hassles, or five events that happened over the past week for ten straight weeks. Guess what happened? The students who wrote five gratitudes were happier and physically healthier. Charles Dickens puts this well: "Reflect upon your present blessings, of which every man has many, not your past misfortunes, of which all men have some."

Those are the Big 7. You know it's important to be happy first, and these are the seven ways to get there. Remember: Just like driving a car, throwing a football, or doing a headstand—you can *learn* to be happier.

6

A final lesson from the convent

A few years ago a group of researchers at the University of Kentucky stumbled upon pure academic gold: cardboard boxes stashed away and full of *handwritten autobiographies* written by nuns as they joined US convents in the 1930s and '40s. So the researchers read these autobiographies and began sorting them into piles based on how positive the attitude and emotion were in each one.

Here are a couple that show the difference between low and high positive emotion:

Sister 1: I was born on September 26, 1909, the eldest of seven children, five girls and two boys. My candidate year was spent in the Motherhouse, teaching Chemistry and Second Year Latin at Notre Dame Institute. With God's grace, I intend to do my best for our Order, for the spread of religion, and for my personal sanctification.

Sister 2: God started my life off well by bestowing upon me a grace of inestimable value. The past year which I have spent as a candidate studying at Notre Dame College has been a very happy one. Now I look forward with eager joy to receiving the Holy Habit of Our Lady and to a life of union with Love Divine.

Pretty different, aren't they?

Turns out it was easy for the researchers to categorize the autobiographies into four "levels of happiness" seventy years later and excitedly rub their hands together, squeal nerdy academic researcher squeals, and compare those dusty old autobiographies with how well the nuns were doing today.

Now, keep in mind the best thing about studying nuns is that all the difficult, hard-to-control variables were controlled. None of them smoked, drank, had sex, got married, or had kids . . . ever! They even lived in the same cities, ate the same foods, and wore the same clothes. (Who's doing a load of whites? Nobody! Ever!)

Therefore, their positive attitude seventy years ago was **the prime indicator** of how long they lived.

That's why this study is so powerful.

And guess what the researchers found out?

Revolutionary findings that sent academic circles buzzing. Staggering takeaways about the power of starting with a positive lens in your life. They published the results and called them "Positive Emotions in Early Life and Longevity: Findings from the Nun Study."

Here's what they found:

- The happiest nuns lived ten years longer than the least happy nuns.
- By age eighty, the most happy group had lost only 25% of its population, whereas the least happy group had lost 60%.
- 54% of the most happy nuns reached the age of ninety-four, compared to 15% of the least happy nuns.

The Nun Study shows an incredibly strong link between how happy you are today and how long you're going to live. And it's not just length, either! Think of it: You will be happier through all those years, too.

Happy people don't have the best of everything.

They make the best of everything.

Be happy first.

BE HAPPY FIRST

Secret #2

Do This

and Criticism

Can't Touch You

1

The only goal you set that matters

Blog Stats: 50,017 hits.

Heart thumping, palms sweating, I sit back on my creaky wooden chair, stare at my blog, and grimace. Is this real? I click Refresh, scrunch my face, and look at the screen again.

Blog Stats: 50,792 hits.

Seven hundred people visited my blog in the last thirty seconds, I think to myself.

Only four weeks ago I'd started writing 1000 Awesome Things, and after a few hundred visits it looks like that day's post—#980 Old, dangerous playground equipment—went viral while I was at work.

My heart beats faster.

I had one simple goal when I started writing 1000 Awesome Things.

I wanted to try to write 1000 awesome things for 1000 days in a row.

But after the first couple weeks writing about broccoflower and potato chip crumbs, I started noticing the stats counter on the side of my page.

It showed how many people had visited. Seven then twenty then *dozens* then *hundreds*. I got hooked on watching the number climb.

So I set a different goal for myself. I decided I wanted fifty thousand hits.

When #980 Old, dangerous playground equipment went viral a few weeks later, I had accomplished my goal.

But then I told myself fifty thousand was too small. Too easy. It didn't mean much getting fifty thousand hits. The big sites had a million. So that became my new goal. One million hits.

I kept writing every day, adding links to email signatures and blog comments I left around the Web. I got stickers printed and started handing them out. I wrote #951 Hearing a stranger fart in public, #933 The first scoop out of a jar of peanut butter, and #909 Bakery air.

Flash-forward a few months later and . . . I got to one million hits!

I enjoyed the feeling for a couple days before realizing the best blogs don't just get a million hits. They get ten million hits and get turned into books and movies. I had set my goal too low. One million hits wasn't *worth* anything. Nothing *happened* when you got a million hits. I needed to go big to get some real action.

So I set a new goal.

Ten million hits.

For six months, I kept writing. After work every day, I got takeout and sat at my computer well into the night. I wrote the next post, responded to email, and started getting interviews with local radio and TV stations. I was featured on the front page of the *Toronto Star*! I wrote #874 The Five Second Rule, #858 The other side of the pillow, and #824 Finding the TV remote after looking forever. Nine months after I had started my blog, I suddenly reached ten million hits, won two awards for Best Blog in the World, and was approached by literary agents to turn my blog into a book.

Once I had a literary agent I started researching the book industry. I learned that more than three hundred thousand books are published in the United States *every single year.* And well over a million a year are published around the world. Suddenly it dawned on me: Getting a book published was not very special. A million people did it every year!

I looked at bestseller lists and they had only ten or twenty books on them. I calculated that only a few hundred books make bestseller lists each year. Less than 0.01%.

So I set a new goal.

I wanted my book to be a bestseller.

I wanted to be one of the 0.01%.

The Globe and Mail published a bestseller list every weekend and I started checking it. What did these books have in common, what made them great, what made them sell?

So for the next year I kept writing my blog every day, writing my book, and working on a book launch plan. My plan was to work with bloggers to prepare interviews and articles about my book while working with my publisher to line up radio, newspaper, and TV interviews—all to come out when the book hit shelves.

Basically, the entire year after winning the awards, I was consumed with *The Book of Awesome* hitting the bestseller list. It was all I wanted, thought about, talked about. Then the big day of publication finally came!

I woke up early and started interview after interview. I posted a special entry called #526 When dreams come true. My voice turned scratchy, bags under my eyes turned black, and I was sleeping three or four hours a night. And then, finally, the next Saturday morning the newspaper came out and . . .

I hit #2 on the bestseller list!

It was a dream come true. I went to bed happy. I had achieved my goal. My publishers were excited, too! Their joy said to keep pushing.

I woke up the next morning and took a closer look at the bestseller list.

My book was listed with a *1* beside it because it had been on the bestseller list for one week. I noticed other books were on the list for twenty or thirty weeks. Staying power. That was more important than being a one-hit wonder. I didn't want to go the rest of my life telling people my book was a bestseller for only one week.

I suddenly realized that popping on the bestseller list was nice . . . but it was nowhere near my true goal. I wanted this book to be bigger. *The New York Times* bestseller list. A *#1* beside my name.

Eventually *The Book of Awesome* hit #1 on the bestseller list and stayed there for five weeks then ten weeks then fifty weeks then one hundred weeks. Foreign publishers translated the book into German, Korean, French, Dutch, and Portuguese. *The Book of Awesome* hit *The New York Times* bestseller list, too. I was on the *Today* show, *The Early Show*, CNN, and the BBC. The producers of *The Office* optioned TV rights to the book and some big film producers optioned the movie rights, too. I got another book deal, then another, then another . . .

And I had done it!

I had finally reached my goal.

I started smiling. Tried to relax. A few days later, after working so hard for three years straight, lying in bed alone in my tiny apartment, getting three or four hours of sleep, eating takeout for every meal, developing black bags under my eyes, and losing touch with friends . . . I suddenly had a realization.

No matter how many external goals I achieved . . . I just kept setting more.

I started realizing that external goals didn't help me become a better person.

Only internal goals did.

2

What's the biggest problem
with external goals?

When I was stressing about my blog and watching hit counters, bestseller lists, and award nominations, I was using *external motivators*. I wasn't doing it for me. *I was doing it for others.* I lost my self-confidence because I started outsourcing it to signals outside my brain, which I couldn't always control. When those signals were positive, I was flying. Lots of emails, piles of comments, and bestseller list rankings lifted me up and kept me going. But when those signs were negative, even relatively negative, I was devastated. Critical comments, a nasty review, and the inevitable slipping off the bestseller list—meant I was a loser.

3

4 simple words that block all criticism

1. Do
2. It
3. For
4. You

Do it for you.

Don't do it for others.

It's hard to compete endlessly because there's always more to compete with when you get there.

Remember we will always be number two to seven billion at everything in the world. And every level we go up has new peers, new benchmarks, new competitors. A CEO once told me, "You always think the geniuses are at the next level."

But the next level never ends unless you are literally *the best in the entire world*. What are the odds of that happening? Well, they are one in seven billion.

You have better chances of getting struck by lightning every single day of your life.

4

Why your dream job could be the worst job you ever have

Teddy Roosevelt famously said, "It is not the critic who counts, not the man who points out how the strong man stumbles, or where the doer of deeds could have done them better. The credit belongs to the man who is actually in the arena, whose face is marred by dust and sweat and blood, who strives valiantly, who errs, who comes short again and again, because there is no effort without error and shortcoming, but who does actually strive to do the deeds, who knows great enthusiasms, the great devotions, who spends himself in a worthy cause, who at the best knows in the end the triumph of high achievement, and who at the worst, if he fails, at least fails while daring greatly, so that his place shall never be with those cold and timid souls who neither know victory nor defeat."

It's not the critic who counts.

But what motivates that man in the arena? Why is he working so hard?

First, remember there are two types of motivation: intrinsic and extrinsic. Intrinsic is internal. You're doing it because you want to. Extrinsic is external. You're doing it because you get something for it.

Guess which gets better performance?

Studies show that when we begin to value the *rewards* we get for doing a task, we lose our inherent interest in doing the task. Like, we *literally* lose interest—as in, the interest we have becomes truly lost in our minds, hidden away from our own brains, as the shiny external reward sits front and center and becomes the new object of our desire.

While at Brandeis University, Dr. Teresa Amabile performed experiments on elementary school and college students and asked groups to make "silly collages" and invent stories for them. Some were told they were getting rewards for their work and some were not. What happened? Based on independent judges, who didn't know who was getting paid, the least creative projects by far were done by students who were promised rewards for their work. Dr. Amabile said, "It may be that commissioned work will, in general, be less creative than work that is done out of pure interest."

Makes sense.

When you're **not doing it for you** . . . you're not doing a good job.

It's not just that getting rewards hurts quality, either.

In another study, seventy-two creative writers at Brandeis and Boston Universities were split into three groups of twenty-four creative writers each and asked to write poetry. Some were given extrinsic reasons for doing so—impressing teachers, making money, getting into fancy grad schools. Others were given a list of intrinsic reasons for writing haiku—enjoying the feeling of expressing themselves, the fun of playing with words. And the third group wasn't given any reasons at all. On the sidelines, Dr. Amabile put together a group of a dozen poet judges, mixed up all the poems, and had the judges evaluate the work.

By far and away, the lowest-quality poems were from those who had the list of extrinsic motivators for doing so.

James Garbarino, former president of the Erikson Institute for Advanced Study in Child Development, was curious about this phenomenon. He studied fifth- and sixth-grade girls hired to tutor younger children. Some of the tutors were offered free movie tickets for doing a good job. Some weren't. What happened? The girls offered free movie tickets took longer to communicate ideas, got frustrated more easily, and did a worse job in the end than the girls who were given nothing except the feeling of helping someone else.

I was surprised by the studies, but they made sense to me.

I remembered writing articles for the *Golden Words* comedy newspaper at Queen's University every Sunday for four straight years while in college. I didn't get paid a cent but loved every minute because I got to hang out with a group of really funny people writing articles that made us all laugh. I loved it so much that I took a job working at a New York City comedy writing startup in my last summer at college. I rented an apartment on the Lower East Side and started working in a Brooklyn loft with writers from *The Simpsons* and *Saturday Night Live.*

Wow, I remember thinking. I can't believe I'm getting paid to do what I love.

It was the hardest job of my life.

Instead of having creative freedom to write whatever I wanted, I had to write "800 words about the bright side of getting dumped by 5:00 p.m." for a client like *Cosmopolitan* magazine. Instead of joking with friends naturally, finding chemistry with certain people, I was scheduled to write with others. Eventually my interest in comedy writing faded and faded and faded . . . and I decided I would never do it for money again.

When I started writing 1000 Awesome Things, I said I'd never put ads on the website. I would have liked the beer money! But I knew the ads would feel like work to me. I might start writing an article to get more views on an ad. And I would be spending time checking invoices. Looking at payment transfers. It would take away—or just hide—my reasons for writing in the first place. I was smart about that . . . but not smart enough to ignore the other extrinsic motivators that kept showing up. Stat counters, website awards, bestseller lists. It was all so visible, so measurable, and so tempting.

I started looking into this whole "extrinsic motivators kill intrinsic motivators" phenomenon and kept finding studies showing this to be true.

Professor Edward Deci of the University of Rochester had students try to solve a puzzle. Some were told they were competing with other students and some were not. Guess what happened? The students who were told they were competing with others simply stopped working once the other kids finished their puzzle—believing themselves to be out of the race. They ran out of reasons to do the puzzle in the first place. But those who weren't told they were competing with others kept going once their peers finished.

When you don't feel like you're competing with others, you compete only with yourself.

You do it for you.

And you do more, go further, and perform better.

Want to hear an old joke?

An old man enjoyed sitting on his front porch every day until the elementary school bell rang and neighborhood kids walking past his porch stopped to taunt him from the sidewalk.

Finally, the old man came up with a plan.

He offered the children a dollar each if they'd return the next day and yell their insults.

They were excited, so they returned, yelled their insults, and he paid each of them a dollar.

He then said he'd like them to come back the next day and yell their insults, but he could pay them only 25 cents.

So they returned, yelled their insults, and he paid them a quarter each.

Before they left, he said that he could only afford to pay them a penny on Wednesday.

"Forget it," they said. "That's not worth it."

And they never bothered him again.

5

The 3 *S*'s of success

How can I be successful?"

I smiled at the eager fifty-something woman beside me. We were sitting at Table 1 at a banquet dinner for SHAD, a non-profit for which I sit on the board of directors, as students paraded across the stage winning awards. Me being a director, she being a sponsor, we would be sitting a foot apart for the next two hours. The chairman of the board introduced us with a big grin and said, "Neil's a *New York Times* bestseller who's sold over a million books! Nancy wants to be a writer! Enjoy!"

Now I was smiling at her bright and shiny face. She spent a few minutes telling me about the years she'd spent writing novels that she's never shown anybody. Then came the big question.

"What's your secret to success?" she asked.

I paused for a minute and thought about it.

"Do you have a pen?" I asked, grabbing a napkin. "Let me show you a scribble."

"There are three *S*'s of Success," I started. "I put them in The Success Triangle. It took me a really long time to figure this out. The first step is actually figuring out what kind of success you want."

Sales success is about sales. Your book is a commercial hit! Everybody's reading it, everybody's talking about it, you're on TV. You sell hundreds then thousands then millions of copies. Your book becomes an "it book." A catchphrase. Dump trucks beep while backing into your garage to pour endless royalty payments.

Social success means you're a success among your peers. People you respect. This is *critical* success. The industry loves you! *The New York Times* reviews your book. You're short-listed for the Man Booker Prize. An influential author you look up to sends you a letter, which feels like gold.

Self success is in your head. It's invisible! Only you know if you have it. Self success means you achieved what you wanted to achieve. For yourself. You're genuinely proud of your accomplishment, you're happy with your work, and, most important, you're *satisfied.* You want nothing. You feel contentment. Some people believe without self success, no amount of sales or social success will ever feel meaningful.

The 3 *S*'s of Success apply to all industries, professions, and aspects of life. Success is not one-dimensional. You must decide what kind of success you want.

Are you in marketing? Sales success means your product flew off the shelves, sales shot through the roof, and your numbers blew away forecasts. Social success means you were written up in prestigious magazines. Nominated for an award. Recognized by the CEO at a company meeting. Self success? That's the same. How do *you* feel about your accomplishments?

Are you a teacher? Sales success means you're offered promotions. Asked if you're interested in becoming vice principal or principal one day. Social success means you're presenting at conferences, mentoring new teachers, and the principal talks about your work. Self success? That's the same. How do *you* feel about your accomplishments?

Here's the catch: It is impossible to have all three successes.

I say this because I've never seen it and I don't think you should aspire toward it. At least at first. If you have one type of success for a very long time, and then you add another for a long time, then sure. Go ahead. Try for the third.

But often two corners of The Success Triangle actually prevent the third.

How so?

Well, sales success can block self success. That's what happened when I got hooked on blog counters and bestseller lists. My personal goals suddenly took a backseat to more tangible commercial goals. Think of Krusty the Clown–brand cough syrup, home pregnancy tests, and imitation gruel. ("Nine out of ten orphans can't tell the difference.") This is the artist who sells out. There's nothing wrong with that! But you can see how commercial success blocks personal success sometimes.

And self success doesn't necessarily have a marketable strategy—so no sales or social success follows. The birthday cakes you bake for your daughter. That incredible lesson you put your heart into for weeks. The backyard deck you built with your bare hands. You wouldn't expect royalty payments or critical reviews from those endeavors. You're not trying to sell cakes, lessons, or decks. You could! But that wasn't your goal.

Lastly, critical darlings rarely sell! Social success can block sales success. Let me give you an example: One of my favorite movies a few years ago was *The Hurt Locker*. Tense, dramatic, I was glued to the screen. The movie won Best Picture at the Academy Awards. There is no higher honor! But its total domestic box office was 17 million dollars. *Alvin and the Chipmunks: The Squeakquel* came out that same year. And it ended up making 219 million dollars.

Which would you have rather made?

Know which of the 3 *S*'s of Success you want.

6

The sad and unfortunate reason
we listen to critics in the first place

We know we shouldn't listen to our critics.

We know we should do things for ourselves.

Morihei Ueshiba, founder of the Japanese martial art aikido, said, "As soon as you concern yourself with the 'good' and 'bad' of your fellows, you create an opening in your heart for maliciousness to enter. Testing, competing with, and criticizing others weaken and defeat you."

So why do we listen? What makes us interested in external measurements? Why do we take outside rankings, results, or opinions over our own opinion of ourselves?

There is a root issue.

An underlying reason.

There is one issue that many of us have, that I know I have, that is at the basis of why we jump at external rankings.

The root issue is . . . our lack of confidence. Self-judgment. We get lost in our own heads, we get confused with mixed advice, so we follow what we see.

The root issue is self-confidence.

And we're going to solve this root issue together in less than ten pages.

"Every single day I come to work I feel like I'm a failure."

Twilight shone through the glass window and dim lights lit up leather chairs and the shiny lacquered desk as I sat staring in disbelief at my Harvard Business School leadership professor as he smiled wryly through wet, shiny eyes.

Tenured Harvard Business School professors have bachelor's degrees, master's degrees, and PhDs, and they finish at the top of their class in all three! They make six-figure salaries and consult and speak on the side to earn even more. And they're teaching at Harvard! A not-too-shabby résumé bullet point.

So why did my Harvard professor consider himself a failure?

"I walk up to my office door every morning and see that the professor in the office to my left has a Nobel Prize . . . and I know I'll never have a Nobel Prize," he continued. "And I see that the professor in the office to my right has written twelve books . . . and I know I'll never write twelve books. I haven't even written one. Every single morning I'm reminded how inferior I am and it kills me."

I looked at him and could tell he was smiling and trying to make a point . . . but I could also see there was some truth in his words. After all, in his world, all his major accomplishments are neutralized by his peers. Piles of degrees, million-dollar bank accounts, prestigious jobs—all just par for the course.

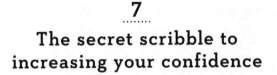

7

The secret scribble to increasing your confidence

What is confidence?
Time for our next scribble.

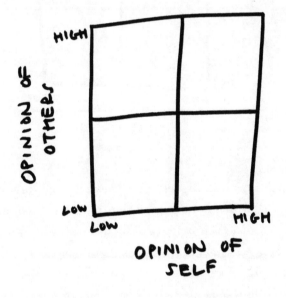

Let's talk about your opinion of yourself. It can be high or low. Sure, it will flip-flop all the time. But let's say in any instant it can be high or it can be low. Does confidence just have to do with your opinion of yourself?

No!

Most people think it does. But we always have an opinion of others, too.

What do you call people with a high opinion of themselves and a low opinion of others?

They're not confident. They are . . .

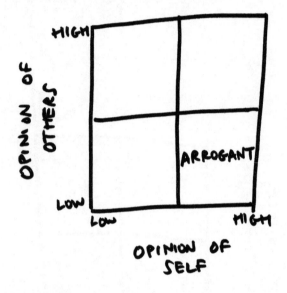

Stuck-up. Egotistical. Bigheaded. Arrogant people are not confident because they don't understand that having a high opinion of others doesn't lower their opinion of themselves. They are affected by other people's confidence! It makes them feel weak. So they try to lower that confidence while increasing their own. Remember the school yard bully who actually feels bad about himself deep down? This is the guy we're talking about here. This is the guy who feels the need to be better than others in order to be good at all.

Next box.

What do you call people with a high opinion of others but a low opinion of themselves?

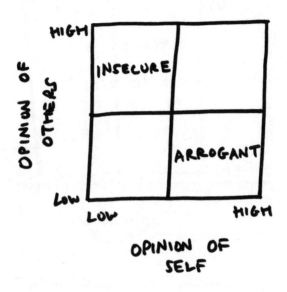

We've all been there! We think greatly of other people and believe ourselves to be "lesser than." You feel this way when you stare at a group photo and say something like "Oh my God! I look hideous! I look huge! You look great, though." Talk about beating yourself up. High opinion of others. Low opinion of yourself.

Insecure.

Now, what do you call people with a low opinion of themselves and a low opinion of others? No high opinions of anyone at all!

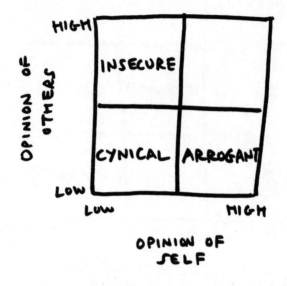

We've all been here, too. Bad days, bad bosses, big mistakes. We can get into a funk and see problems everywhere. We become cynical. The cynic isn't confident. Cynical is the furthest thing from confident! As Conan O'Brien said on his final episode hosting *The Tonight Show*, "All I ask of you is one thing: Please don't be cynical. I hate cynicism—it's my least favorite quality and it doesn't lead anywhere."

What's left?

What do the truly confident people have?

They have a high opinion of themselves. And! They have a high opinion of others.

That is the true definition of confidence.

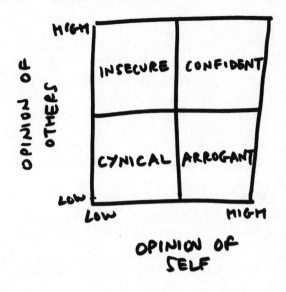

Buddha says, "You can search throughout the entire universe for someone who is more deserving of your love and affection than you are yourself and that person is not to be found anywhere. You yourself, as much as anybody in the entire universe, deserve your love and affection."

8

3 simple steps to self-acceptance

How do we get to that dream place?

How do we accept ourselves and think highly of others at the same time?

How can we separate those two opinions in our mind so we can allow both?

There are three steps to achieving a high opinion of yourself. It is a torturous path! But we go through this journey with every part of ourselves that we eventually learn to accept.

The three steps are:

1. Hide
2. Apologize
3. Accept

And here's what it looks like.

Hide

For years after I graduated from Harvard I answered the question the same way most of my classmates did.

> THEM: So where did you go to school, anyway?
> ME: Boston.
> THEM: Cool.

Eventually, I started realizing that *masking* is a form of self-judgment. I wasn't confident about having attended Harvard. I was afraid to mention Harvard because I was afraid of people's perceptions. Elite, nerdy, trust-fund kids with silver spoons, shady bankers corrupting society—whatever they were going to think, I was going to avoid. Rather than identify with this part of my identity, I hid it. I didn't mention it in my biography, in my blog or any of my books, in any radio lead-ins, any newspaper interviews. I didn't list my degree in my email signature at work like my coworkers.

I called this humility.

But it was fear.

After a couple years, I figured this out and decided that from then on I would tell anybody exactly where I went to school if they asked. Of course, I did this in a tentative way. An awkward way. Like dipping my toe in freezing cold water off the dock. Not really sure. How did I do it?

Apologize

THEM: So where did you go to school, anyway?
ME: (grimacing) Uh . . . Harvard?
THEM: Oh, uh, okay, haha . . . yeah, I heard of the place!
　　Haha, uh . . .

By acting awkward, I made things awkward for others. By apologizing for myself, I forced others to apologize, too.

Eventually, I started realizing that *apologizing* was a form of self-judgment, too. Great, another one!

Apologizing was communicating a part of myself, then immediately sounding a bright red *Family Feud* triple-*X* buzzer through it.

"We surveyed a hundred people and the top five answers are on the board. Name a school you attended."

"Uh . . . Harvard?"

NNNNNNN!

Apologizing avoids ownership.

Apologizing creates distance.

Apologizing suggests a mistake.

Apologizing is what you do when your dog craps on the neighbor's lawn and then you look up and notice your neighbor watching from the window. (Sorry!)

Well, eventually I realized this, and after a couple years of apologizing I finally moved on to the third and final step.

Accept

THEM: So where did you go to school, anyway?

ME: Harvard.

THEM: Cool.

Gone went the tendency to hide the truth from others . . . which reflected my desire to hide it from myself.

Gone went the tentativeness and questioning . . . which reflected my tentativeness and questioning part of myself.

Replacing both came a clear and simple truth. Replacing both came a solid, grounded fact. By being clear and simple, without pretension, without assumptions, I consciously remove myself from any possible judgment that comes from any given statement.

This allows whatever judgment that comes to be wholly owned by the other person.

Physicist Richard Feynman said, "You have no responsibility to live up to what other people think you ought to accomplish. I have no responsibility to be like they expect me to be. It's their mistake, not my failing."

Accepting yourself communicates confidence.

Accepting yourself insulates you from the washing machine of emotions that comes from other people's views swaying your own. Swishing your thoughts. Bending your beliefs. Until they're muddy in even your own head.

What do you do with their views? How do you stop judging yourself?

Laugh at it.

A big laugh helps you look deep, notice your self-judgments, and push through the steps to accepting part of yourself.

H—Hide
A—Apologize
A—Accept

We're all full of self-judgments.

We're fat, lazy, don't exercise enough, aren't worthy of a raise, aren't worthy of her love, wouldn't find another job if we were fired, wouldn't find a new boyfriend if we were dumped. Sometimes we forget that we are all trying, trying, trying. We are all trying. We are all trying. We are all getting better.

You are what you are what you are.

Find what's hidden, stop apologizing, and accept yourself.

9

How does Buddha use this secret?

One day Buddha was visiting a tiny village.

He had become a religious man, also called a Brahman, and was traveling from town to town to share his message. He was becoming so popular that when people heard the Buddha was coming they went to hear him speak. As a result many other Brahmans lost their audience.

One Brahman was so upset with the Buddha that he found him and went to see him late at night. He was furious! "You have no right teaching others," he shouted. "You are as stupid as everyone else. You are nothing but a fake!"

Buddha smiled at the Brahman and listened until he was done with his rant.

When the Brahman was done, Buddha still sat, smiling at him. This made the Brahman even angrier. "Why are you just sitting there smiling? What do you have to say?"

Then Buddha spoke.

"Tell me something, Brahman: Do friends and colleagues, relatives and kinsmen, ever come to your house as guests?"

"Yes," the Brahman answered.

"And tell me something, Brahman," Buddha continued. "Do you serve them foods and delicacies when they arrive?"

"Yes," the Brahman answered, "I do."

"And tell me something, Brahman," Buddha continued. "If they don't accept them, to whom do those foods belong?"

"Well, I suppose if they don't accept them, those foods are all mine."

"Yes," said Buddha. "In the same way, Brahman, I do not accept your anger and your criticism. It is all yours."

The Brahman was stunned and could think of nothing to say.

His anger continued to bubble up inside him, but he had nowhere to put it.

Nobody was accepting it or taking it from him.

Buddha continued: "That with which you have insulted me, who is not insulting, that with which you have taunted me, who is not taunting, that with which you have berated me, who is not berating, that I don't accept from you. It's all yours, Brahman. It's all yours.

"If you become angry with me and I do not get insulted, then the anger falls back on you. You are then the only one who becomes unhappy. All you have done is hurt yourself. If you want to stop hurting yourself, you must get rid of your anger and become loving instead.

"Whoever returns insult to one who is insulting, returns taunts to one who is taunting, returns a berating to one who is berating, is eating together, sharing company, with that person. But I am neither eating together nor sharing your company, Brahman. It's all yours. It's all yours."

10

What does a message secretly hidden under Wimbledon's Centre Court show us?

There are two lines of a poem above the player entrance to Centre Court at Wimbledon:

If you can meet with Triumph and Disaster
And treat those two impostors just the same.

Picture walking down the tunnel and under that sign on your way to play in the Wimbledon final.

Sunlight beams through the entryway and you catch a glimpse of thousands filling the stands. The Royal Family is in their private box, and cameras capture your every action. Smile at your girlfriend, miss a shot and scream, sweat through your T-shirt—it's all beamed to hundreds of millions around the world.

You have played tennis every single day for fifteen years. You picked up an old racquet as a kid and everyone said you were a natural, so you made it your life. Your parents mortgaged their house to get you private lessons. You skipped graduation and prom because of tournaments. You managed to avoid major injuries by designing your off-court life to complement tennis: no skiing, no boozing, no building decks with your hands.

It all led to this. Right here. Right now. This is the big one.

If you win this match, you walk away with 3 million dollars. Lose and you don't. And the 3 million dollars doesn't include the notoriety, sponsorships, and legacy you'll create. Everybody remembers who wins Wimbledon. Nobody remembers who finishes second.

Who are you up against in this game?

Only the best tennis player in the entire world.

Now, right before you walk onto the court, onto the biggest tennis match of your life, your eye catches this quote.

If you can meet with Triumph and Disaster
And treat those two impostors just the same.

It jolts you. You pause and digest it.

No matter what happens right now, Triumph or Disaster, it's an impostor. You should treat them the same. Winning or losing is the same. Place the game in the context of your entire life. The world will go on. You will have more highs and lows no matter what. "If you can meet with Triumph or Disaster, And treat those two impostors just the same."

You are competing only with yourself.

You relax, take a deep breath, and walk on the court smiling.

Although there's no attribution on that wall, these two lines are from a poem called "If—," written by Rudyard Kipling in 1895. Kipling was an English short-story writer and poet born in India who went on to win the Nobel Prize in Literature and was declared England's favorite poet in national polls.

"If—" is thirty-two beautiful lines written by Rudyard Kipling to his son John as parental advice on how to be confident, accept yourself, and do it for you.

"If—" by Rudyard Kipling

If you can keep your head when all about you
Are losing theirs and blaming it on you,
If you can trust yourself when all men doubt you,
But make allowance for their doubting too;
If you can wait and not be tired by waiting,
Or being lied about, don't deal in lies,
Or being hated, don't give way to hating,
And yet don't look too good, nor talk too wise:

If you can dream—and not make dreams your master;
If you can think—and not make thoughts your aim;
If you can meet with Triumph and Disaster
And treat those two impostors just the same;
If you can bear to hear the truth you've spoken
Twisted by knaves to make a trap for fools,

Or watch the things you gave your life to, broken,
And stoop and build 'em up with worn-out tools:

If you can make one heap of all your winnings
And risk it on one turn of pitch-and-toss,
And lose, and start again at your beginnings
And never breathe a word about your loss;
If you can force your heart and nerve and sinew
To serve your turn long after they are gone,
And so hold on when there is nothing in you
Except the Will which says to them: "Hold on!"

If you can talk with crowds and keep your virtue,
Or walk with Kings—nor lose the common touch,
If neither foes nor loving friends can hurt you,
If all men count with you, but none too much;
If you can fill the unforgiving minute
With sixty seconds' worth of distance run,
Yours is the Earth and everything that's in it,
And—which is more—you'll be a Man, my son!

Remember Secret #2. What do you do so criticism can't touch you?

Remember to do it for you.

11

"I don't stand back and judge . . . I do."

D o it for you.

When I was young I asked my cousin why it seemed to me that the NCAA Final Four was more exciting to watch than the NBA. "I don't understand," I said. "These college guys are running as fast as possible, diving for balls, jumping for difficult shots, smiling and laughing the whole time. When I flip to an NBA game the point guard is *walking* up the court. Everyone is *sitting* on the bench instead of standing and screaming." He smiled and said, "The college guys aren't getting paid for it. They might never get paid for it. They're doing it for themselves. Because they love it."

His words rang clear as a bell.

At around that same age I used to love rolling up my parents' change so they could take it to the bank every few months. I loved sorting the coins and counting out the exact number for each roll. I loved standing the coins up on their sides while squeezing them tightly together with my fingers. I loved carefully rolling them into those slippery little papers before folding tightly at the ends. Turning a big jar of coins into a small, heavy pile was deeply satisfying.

Then one day my mom said, "Neil, for your allowance you can keep ten percent of whatever you roll." What did I do? I rolled all the quarters and dimes but quit before the nickels and pennies. I said I'd get back to those. My mom was disappointed. Suddenly I didn't appreciate rolling fifty pennies for five cents when a roll of quarters earned me a dollar.

Do it for you.

Blog counters, score sheets, and job evaluations will always tell you how you're doing. They will deliver external rewards like money, promotions, or critical praise. But those rewards mask your intrinsic motivators. You go from running down the court to walking. You start focusing on appealing to those judging you. Risk-taking disappears.

Remember, it's not the critic who counts. It's the man in the arena. Pick the type of success you're aiming for and have a high opinion of yourself and a high opinion of others along the way. Move through hiding and apologizing to eventually accepting all parts of you. And as Buddha said, let others keep their criticism for you.

Do it for you.

Let's finish this secret with a story.

John Lennon was one of the most fiercely independent artists of all time. Do it for you? He did. Most people who experienced his level of sales and social success would never walk away from the Beatles—but he privately told Paul, George, and Ringo in September 1969 that he was leaving the group. More than a decade later, just weeks before his death, John Lennon was asked in a famous *Playboy* interview if he thought his post-Beatles music would ever have the lasting imprint of his work with the Beatles.

Tough question.

What did he say?

"I'm not judging whether 'I Am the Walrus' is better or worse than 'Imagine.' It is for others to judge. I am doing it. I do. I don't stand back and judge . . . I do."

Say "I do."

Do it for you.

BE HAPPY FIRST
DO IT FOR YOU

Secret #3

The Three Words

That Will Save

You on Your

Very Worst Days

1
....
The first war you
are fighting every day

We are going to get to those three words.

But first we need to understand what's causing our very worst days.

Your amygdala is in the oldest part of your brain. It is responsible for scanning the world for worries. It's a problem-scanning machine. Imagine, you have a problem-scanning machine, right in your head, always on, always scanning, all day and all night. When the machine finds a problem, or even thinks it finds a problem, it flushes your body full of adrenaline and stress hormones, sending you into fight-or-flight mode.

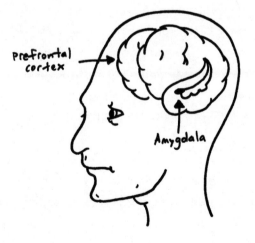

Daniel Goleman, bestselling author of *Emotional Intelligence* says, "The emotional component evolved very early: Do I eat it, or does it eat me?" He calls this the Amygdala Hijack and describes it as a way our brains take control of our bodies.

Remember the reason it's so hard to be happy from Secret #1. We all have negative thoughts. Those negative thoughts helped keep us safe and led to our survival through very strong emotional reactions. See a saber-toothed tiger suddenly look at you from a few hundred feet away in the grassy plains? You need your problem-scanning machine to flash! You have a problem. And this part of our brains is still part of our heads. Part of our lives. Even though the chances of being chased down by two-thousand-pound cats is gone.

This war in our heads reminds us of one major truth, though.

None of us can control our emotions. We can only control our reactions to our emotions.

In addition to the amygdala, our brains have also evolved a prefrontal cortex responsible for rational thought. This is a new part of our brains! This part of our brains contains our most complex thoughts. Let's call it our serenity-now mood tape. It plays quiet music, it contemplates, it's responsible for thinking before acting. It decides what we do before we do it. The prefrontal cortex helps you think things through. It's responsible for language and your ability to solve complex problems.

Sometimes you can feel the problem-scanning machine and your serenity-now mood tape blasting full volume at the same time. Say you get asked to make a presentation to the CEO late one afternoon. Your problem-scanning machine suddenly flashes bright red lights and makes that annoying alarm-clock morning buzz. NN! NN! NN! Meanwhile, your serenity-now mood tape is playing birds chirping and waves crashing onto the beach. That is your brain taking time to decide what to do, trying to think things through, instead of acting on impulses.

It is a war waged inside your own head.

Our problem-scanning machine (amygdala) and our serenity-now mood tape (prefrontal cortex) are at war.

2

The second war you are fighting every day

The second war is the war between **more** and **enough**.

Today we live in a Culture of More instead of our old Culture of Enough.

New trend? No. Growing trend. Growing in our culture for more than a hundred years.

Pop Momand was one of the first to put a finger on our shift from the Culture of Enough to the Culture of More. Pop was born in San Diego on May 15, 1887, and moved to New York City at age twenty-one, where he got a job as a sketch artist for *The New York World*. After getting married, Pop had a bit of success under his belt, so he and his wife moved to Cedarhurst, New York—a suburb on Long Island with big homes and moneymakers. Though the Momands had a high quality of life, Pop and his wife found themselves in a constant race to have an even higher quality of life than their wealthier neighbors. It drained them! So they quit the fancy lifestyle, moved back to Manhattan, and got an apartment in a poor part of town. Then Pop created a comic strip based on his experience in the ritzy burbs and pitched it to his bosses.

The comic strip he created was called *Keeping Up with the Joneses*. (He originally called it *Keeping Up with the Smiths* but changed it because *Joneses* sounded better.) Pop told the story of the fictional McGinnises, whose obsession with high society dominates their lives. The Joneses are a couple the reader never sees—a comic-book Polkaroo—but they wave a commanding wand over the McGinnises' lives.

Here's the very first *Keeping Up with the Joneses* strip ever published, more than a hundred years ago, in 1913:

KEEPING UP WITH THE JONESES.

—BY POP.

Punchy, acerbic, reflecting society's growing obsession with relative wealth, the strip took off, getting syndicated and picked up in hundreds of newspapers and eventually running for *twenty-eight years*. It was even turned into a book, a movie, and a musical.

Meg Jacobs writes in *Technology and Culture* about the growth of the Culture of More between 1890 and 1930:

"As new technologies enabled mass production and mass distribution, Americans no longer had to just be content with what they had; they could act on their desires. No longer a sin, envy was now a staple of the new consumer economy."

Americans no longer had to be just content with what they had. They could act on their desires!

After World War I there were new mass production techniques that enabled mass marketing of products like washing machines, stoves, and canned goods that advertised convenience. Who didn't want one? And along came installment buying for large items like houses. Suddenly we had radios to beam advertisements right into our houses. Buying things was driving the economy!

"We must shift America from a needs to a desires culture," wrote Paul Mazur of Lehman Brothers in a 1927 issue of *Harvard Business Review*. "People must be trained to desire, to want new things, even before the old have been entirely consumed. We must shape a new mentality in America. Man's desires must overshadow his needs."

More, more, we all want more.

We have grown up in a world where more has always meant better. But that's baloney! More than a hundred years later and we are still *Keeping Up with the Joneses.*

A couple years ago I asked my boss Mike how his young kids were doing as I was packing up my notes and leaving his office on a late Friday afternoon before the weekend. He was head of the department and had the only office at the company with abstract paintings on the walls and leather chairs beside his desk.

"Good, good, thanks. They're excited to show me an app tonight which they built at school."

"Oh, that's cool." I looked up. "Do they have their own laptops?"

"Yeah." He smiled at me, looking a bit guilty.

He saw my quiet smile back and continued.

"Look, my kids are lucky . . . you and I both know that. But they don't. Their world is different. We live in a big house, they go to private schools, they have their own computers. But their friends at school go to Europe for long weekends and we don't do that. And one has an indoor basketball court in his house. My son came home from school yesterday and asked me why we didn't have a basketball court inside our house."

The Culture of More affects us all!

So what do we do?

3

The one thing many billionaires
want but cannot have

Your problem-scanning machine spends its day looking for worries. It's helpful when you're in serious trouble but stressful when you're not. On top of that, we're living in a Culture of More versus a Culture of Enough. Everywhere we look, we are reminded of what else we need. You can move to a shack in the woods to get away from it all! But we'd miss you too much there. Please don't do that.

Bottom line: It's tough playing defense against those wars—so where do you start?

First, you need to remember the one thing most billionaires want but cannot have.

Kurt Vonnegut and Joseph Heller are two of the most famous authors of the twentieth century, writers of classics that have sold millions, including *Slaughterhouse-Five* and *Catch-22*. They were friends, and there's an old story Kurt Vonnegut wrote in *The New Yorker* after Joseph Heller passed away:

> *True story, Word of Honor:*
> *Joseph Heller, an important and funny writer*
> *now dead,*
> *and I were at a party given by a billionaire*
> *on Shelter Island.*

I said, "Joe, how does it make you feel
to know that our host only yesterday
may have made more money
than your novel 'Catch-22'
has earned in its entire history?"
And Joe said, "I've got something he can never have."
And I said, "What on earth could that be, Joe?"
And Joe said, "The knowledge that I've got enough."
Not bad! Rest in peace!

4

What does a Greek philosopher have in common with the Rolling Stones?

Greek philosopher Epictetus says, "Wealth consists not in having great possessions, but in having few wants."

A famous Persian proverb hung on my aunt's kitchen wall reads, "I cried because I had no shoes, until I met a man who had no feet."

And the Rolling Stones sing, "You can't, always get, what you wa-ant. You can't, always get, what you wa-ant. You can't, always get, what you wa-ant. But if you try sometimes, you just might find— you get what you neeeeeeeeeeeeed."

5

When does making a million dollars feel like nothing?

Thinking about the trouble we get into when we fall into the Culture of More reminds me of a dinner conversation I had with my friend Josh Tannehill. Josh was asked by his company to move from CEO to an advisory role, which meant he was going from making a couple million a year to half of that. Still a great job. Just a lower-level position than he had before. Less responsibilities. Less than what he wanted.

I asked Josh over dinner how he was feeling about the new job.

"I'll be honest," he said. "I'm worried about making ends meet. Donna's running a design store that loses money but gives her so much joy. We're halfway through building our retirement home north of San Francisco and the invoices keep getting bigger. Plus there's our place on Martha's Vineyard. Our whole family meets there for Fourth of July and Thanksgiving. With the amount of moving we've done for work, it's become our home. But the boats, taxes, and maintenance are too much. With two kids in grad school and our oldest needing financial support, I honestly don't know what to do."

I felt sorry for Josh. He was in pain. He was an unfortunate example of what the Culture of More can do.

What's the solution?

It's time for the three words.

1. Remember
2. The
3. Lottery

Remember the lottery.

What does that mean?

It means be conscious of your problem-scanning machine's Amygdala Hijack, be conscious of the more you want, and be conscious to remember how lucky you are to be where you are. Remember you have enough! Remember more isn't always better.

Remember the lottery.

6

The classic tale of the Mexican fisherman

A boat is docked in a tiny fishermen's village.
A tourist wearing expensive sunglasses and a fancy watch walks by and compliments a fisherman on the quality of his fish and asks how long it took him to catch them.

"Not very long," answers the fisherman.

"But then, why didn't you stay out longer and catch more?" asks the tourist.

The fisherman explains his small catch is enough to meet his needs and those of his family.

The tourist asks, "But what do you do with the rest of your time?"

"I sleep late, fish a little, play with my children, and take a siesta with my wife. In the evenings, I go into the village to see my friends, have a few drinks, play the guitar, and sing a few songs. I have a full life."

The tourist jumps in. "I have an MBA and I can help you! You should start by fishing longer every day. You can then sell the extra fish you catch. With the extra money, you can buy a bigger boat."

"And after that?" asks the fisherman.

"With the extra money the larger boat will bring, you can buy a second one and a third one and so on until you have an entire fleet of trawlers. Instead of selling your fish to a middleman, you can then negotiate directly with the processing plants and maybe even open your own plant. You can then leave this little village and move to New York City! From there you can direct your huge new enterprise."

"How long would that take?" asks the fisherman.

"Twenty or twenty-five years, at most," replies the tourist.

"And after that?"

"After that? Well, my friend, that's when it gets really interesting," answers the tourist, laughing. "When your business gets really big, you can sell your company stock to the public and make millions!"

"Millions? Really? And after that?" asks the fisherman.

"After that you'll be able to retire, live in a tiny village near the coast, sleep late, play with your children, catch a few fish, take a siesta with your wife, and spend your evenings drinking and playing guitar with your friends."

7

How to use the three words
on your very worst days

The Mexican fisherman already had enough. He didn't need to remember the lottery. He knew he'd already won!

You and I aren't so lucky. I used to feel stress several times a week. When the car in front of me didn't move on a green, when I dropped and shattered a glass on the kitchen floor, when I had a deadline coming up next week. I felt like my life was on the line. I felt frustrated if everything wasn't going right.

What did I do?

Remember the lottery.

In these moments I moved my head to a zoomed out state.

When I was a kid I lay in bed picturing my body slowly floating up and up and up over my bed and my room and my house. Then I'd picture floating even higher, above the neighborhood and the city and the clouds into low-orbit outer space. I would gaze down at the distant flickering lights of my hometown. And I'd imagine my problems way down there. And nothing felt as serious.

Remember the lottery.

So let's try this together. How small does Earth look next to Uranus and Neptune and Saturn and Jupiter? Well, if we are a golf ball, they are tennis balls and bowling balls. And how big is the sun compared to our golf ball? It's larger than a house!

And as we keep zooming out there are hundreds of thousands of stars just like our sun filling up our Milky Way galaxy. What's a galaxy? A clump of stars, gas, and dust held together by gravity. We live in one, and scientists estimate there are six hundred thousand stars in our galaxy alone.

Yes, our sun is just one of six hundred thousand stars in our galaxy. We are all spinning out there! But it goes much farther. How much farther? Well, have you seen this before?

It's the Hubble Space Telescope. Basically the world's biggest camera. It was invented to take pictures of outer space *from* outer space. We blasted it off more than twenty years ago, pointed it into the deepest darkest corner of the universe, and opened the shutter for a few months. Then we closed the shutter, pulled the camera back to Earth, got the picture developed, and guess what came back?

I think it's the most beautiful photo ever taken.

Every single one of those bright specks in the picture on the following page is *an entire galaxy.* Every single one of those specks is another collection of hundreds of thousands of stars.

And there is nowhere else in the deep distant universe where our species exists. Nowhere else we can breathe air, drink water, eat plants. Nowhere else we can find people to meet, fall in love, and make babies.

We live on the only place that can possibly support life.

Carl Sagan said, "It has been said that astronomy is a humbling and character-building experience. There is perhaps no better demonstration of the folly of human conceits than this distant image of our tiny world. To me, it underscores our responsibility to deal more kindly with one another, and to preserve and cherish the pale blue dot, the only home we've ever known."

We live on the pale blue dot. And it's a beautiful dot. So on this planet, on the only planet in the universe where we can live, we *get to be alive*. You have to remember that most people who have ever lived on Earth are dead.

There are about 7 billion people on Earth today and 115 billion people who have ever lived in the history of the world. That means 108 billion people are dead. Most people have already lived their lives. Put another way: Fourteen out of every fifteen people who have *ever lived* will never see another sunset again, have a bowl of chocolate ice cream, or kiss their kids good night. Fourteen out of every fifteen people will never stroll by the smell of their neighbor barbecuing, flip to the cold side of the pillow before sleeping in on a Sunday, or blow out the flickering candles of a birthday cake in a dark kitchen surrounded by their closest friends.

Being alive means you've already won the lottery.

You are among the wealthiest people in the entire world. The average world income is five thousand dollars. Are you higher than that? Then you're in the top 50%. And if you're higher than fifty thousand dollars you're in the top 0.5%. Do you need much more than 99.5% of people alive? You either have the money to buy this book or you have the time to read it. Either way, you have it good!

You already have more than almost everybody on the planet.

On your very worst days, you have to push your negative thoughts. You have to take a step back. You have to remember the lottery.

Because you've already won.

BE HAPPY FIRST

DO IT FOR YOU

REMEMBER THE LOTTERY

Do Anything

I wish I'd had the courage to live a life true to myself, not the life others expected of me.

—THE NUMBER ONE REGRET OF THE DYING,
REPORTED BY A PALLIATIVE NURSE
IN *THE GUARDIAN*

Remembering that I'll be dead soon is the most important tool I've ever encountered to help me make the big choices in life. Because almost everything—all external expectations, all pride, all fear of embarrassment or failure—these things just fall away in the face of death, leaving only what is truly important. Remembering that you are going to die is the best way I know to avoid the trap of thinking you have something to lose. You are already naked. There is no reason not to follow your heart.

—STEVE JOBS

Remind yourself. Nobody built like you. You design yourself.

—JAY Z

Secret #4

The Dream We
All Have That Is
Completely Wrong

1

The terrible tragedy of Mr. Wilson

He's dead."

Staring in shock at my high school Guidance Department secretary, I thought that it couldn't be true. I'd just talked to him last week.

"It happened so suddenly," she whispered, tears shining through thick glasses, glossy red lips quivering silently in slow motion. "I am so sorry."

Mr. Wilson was my guidance counselor. He had a shiny head holding two fluffy-cloud patches of gray hair on the sides and wore thick glasses and loose-fitting gray T-shirts while helping students with timetables, college applications, and personal problems.

Everybody loved Mr. Wilson.

I talked to him about summer jobs and he calmed me down during exams. He had a quiet, big-picture worldview that helped us get above ourselves and see beyond life in our hometown.

You could tell Mr. Wilson loved his job by the way his eyes twinkled as he bounced through the halls, spouting hellos and high-fiving students, calling everybody by name. He was always smiling, and our school was his home.

Back when I was in high school, the government had mandatory retirement. You turned sixty-five and poof! The government yanked you out of the workforce in a cloud of smoke and moved you straight on to old-age pension. You had no choice. And let's face it—almost everybody wanted to retire way before sixty-five, anyway. TV ads preached "Freedom 55" with gray-haired couples skipping town to swim at the cottage, play golf, and sail into the sunset.

Retirement is a good thing. A great thing! What everybody wants, dreams about, wishes for, over and over and over and over . . . until it finally comes.

Do whatever, whenever, wherever . . . forever?

Sounds like a good deal!

The funny thing is that when Mr. Wilson retired . . . he didn't look happy. None of us did. We had the big celebration with cake, music from the band, and teary speeches from former students. It was like the final scene in *Mr. Holland's Opus*. Mr. Wilson said he was excited to be retiring, but his thin smile and wet eyes said the opposite.

But mandatory retirement came at age sixty-five . . . and so he retired.

The next week he had a heart attack and died.

2

Thomas Jefferson and Teddy Roosevelt agree on this

Thomas Jefferson said, "Determine never to be idle. No person will have occasion to complain of the want of time, who never loses any."

Teddy Roosevelt said, "The best prize that life has to offer is the chance to work hard at work worth doing."

Former *Esquire* editor Martha Sherrill said, "I often think about dogs when I think about work and retirement. There are many breeds of dog that just need to be working, and useful, or have a job of some kind, in order to be happy. Otherwise they are neurotically barking, scratching, or tearing up the sofa. A working dog needs to work. And I am a working dog."

So what kind of dog are you?

If you like thinking, if you like trying, if you like creating, if you like teaching, if you like learning, if you like connecting, then chances are good you're a working dog, too. And what do working dogs do?

They work.

They never give up.

They never stop doing.

They never retire.

If you like neurotically barking, scratching, and tearing up the sofa, let's chat. Because the truth is, you always need to do something. Something different, something interesting, something you love.

But let me tell you another secret.

You need an ikigai first.

3

What can the healthiest one-hundred-year-olds in the world teach us?

Men and women in Okinawa live an average of *seven years* longer than Americans and have the longest disability-free life expectancy on Earth. Ancient Chinese legends call these sandy islands popping out of the sparkling blue East China Sea "the land of the immortals." This is where a ninety-six-year-old defeated a former boxing champ in his thirties. This is where a 105-year-old killed a poisonous snake with a flyswatter. There are more people over a hundred years old there than anywhere.

Researchers from *National Geographic* were so fascinated by Okinawans that they studied what helped them live so long. What did they find out? They eat off smaller plates, they stop eating when they're 80% full, and they have a beautiful setup where they're put into social groups as babies to slowly grow old together.

But they also have an outlook on life that is very different from ours in the West. While we think of retirement as the golden age of putting greens, cottage docks, and staring at the clouds, guess what they call retirement in Okinawa?

They don't!

They don't even have a word for retirement.

Literally nothing in their language describes the concept of stopping work completely.

Instead, they have the word *ikigai* (pronounced like "icky guy"), which roughly means "the reason you wake up in the morning." You can think of it as the thing that drives you most.

In Okinawa there is a 102-year-old karate master whose ikigai is to carry forth his martial art, a 100-year-old fisherman whose ikigai is to feed his family, a 102-year-old woman whose ikigai is to hold her great-great-great-granddaughter.

Sound bunk?

Well, Toshimasa Sone and his colleagues at the Tohoku University Graduate School of Medicine thought it might be—so they put the ikigai concept to a test. They spent seven years in Sendai, Japan, studying the longevity of more than forty-three thousand Japanese adults, looking at age, gender, education, body mass index, cigarette use, alcohol consumption, exercise, employment, perceived stress, history of disease, and even subjects' self-rated scores of how healthy they were. Then they asked every single one of these forty-three thousand people: "Do you have an ikigai in your life?"

Can you guess what they found out?

Participants reporting an ikigai at the beginning of the study were more likely to be married, educated, and employed. They had higher levels of self-rated health and lower levels of stress.

What about at the end of the seven-year study?

95% of folks with an ikigai were alive!

Only 83% of those without an ikigai made it that long.

So guess what I gave Leslie for Christmas last year?

An ikigai card. I made two cards out of construction paper, folded them up, and put one on each of our bedside tables. They cost me about ten cents. We each wrote down our ikigai and left the cards on our bedsides. She wrote "To turn young minds into future leaders," and I wrote "To remind myself and others how lucky we are to be alive." We leave the cards on our nightstands so we're reminded of them first thing in the morning. We change what they say sometimes. I changed my ikigai to "Finish writing *The Happiness Equation*" for a while.

Why do we have these ikigais?

They are a reason to get up in the morning.

With an ikigai card when you wake up . . . you know where you're going.

4

The single greatest lesson we can learn from *Alice's Adventures in Wonderland*

The ikigai idea of having a purpose reminds me of my favorite quote from Lewis Carroll's *Alice's Adventures in Wonderland*:

> One day Alice came to a fork in the road and saw a Cheshire cat in a tree.
>
> "Which road do I take?" she asked.
>
> "Where do you want to go?" was his response.
>
> "I don't know," Alice answered.
>
> "Then," said the cat, "it doesn't matter."

5

The horrible idea the Germans had that ruined things for everybody

Where did retirement even come from? No purpose, no ikigai? It doesn't matter which way you go if you don't know where you're going.

Sure, we all have bad days at work. Bosses agitate, coworkers frustrate. But work gives us purpose, belonging, and direction. Retirement plucks us out of the spinning gears of the world and drops our withered bones off at the beach. Now you're nowhere, with nothing to do and nowhere to go. Ever again!

Why did we think this was a good idea?

Who came up with this plan?

The Germans.

Yes, it was their invention of retirement completely out of the blue in 1889 that established the concept for all of us. Retirement was meant to free up jobs for young people by paying those sixty-five years and older to do nothing till they died.

But there was one big difference between 1889 Germany and the world we live in today.

The average life span was sixty-seven years old.

"Those who are disabled from work by age and invalidity have a well-grounded claim to care from the state," said Otto von Bismarck, chancellor of Germany, in 1889. Given retirement age and average life span were two years apart, that was easy for him to say. Penicillin wasn't discovered for another forty years!

Otto ended up setting an arbitrary world standard for retirement age at sixty-five. The number had no significance other than its proximity to the age people died. Other developed countries kept following suit in the years to follow, which brings us to today.

Harold Koenig is an expert on retirement. A table from his *Purpose and Power in Retirement* shows the percentage of men *over* age sixty-five still working by year:

1880 − 78%
1900 − 65%
1920 − 60%
1930 − 58%
1940 − 42%
1960 − 31%
1980 − 25%
2000 − 16%

Here is an excerpt from his history of retirement painted in his excellent book:

> At first, retirement—especially forced retirement—was viewed negatively by a significant proportion of the American population. Some studies indicated that 50–60 percent of those over age sixty-five would continue working if retirement could be deferred . . . "Activity theory" argued that retirement was a violation of older persons' need for social and occupational integration . . .
>
> After World War II, older persons in America became

more and more a generation separate from the rest of a society that did not value them or their contributions. Young adults, who in the past often lived, raised their families, and worked near their parents' homes, were becoming increasingly mobile because of jobs that frequently took them to a different state or across the country. At the same time, older adults were becoming more financially secure because of pensions and entitlement programs. They were also living longer and having better health because of advances in medicine and healthier lifestyles. Because of increased finances and improved health, older adults began to rely less and less on children and other family members. It was into this "cultural vacuum," says [author Marc] Freedman, that the leisure entrepreneurs stepped in to offer older adults their vision of the "golden years."

The first inkling of such efforts were seen in 1951 when the Corning Corporation had a roundtable discussion in which a national marketing campaign was proposed to educate people over fifty about how to enjoy leisure. The strategy was to glamorize leisure and to make every older adult feel like he or she had a right to it. Insurance companies, deeply involved in the pension business, got into the act by mass advertisement of retirement preparation classes that encouraged separation from society and focused on consumption and self-preoccupation. This began the transformation of retirement as a time of rest, relaxation, and fun that every American would look forward to as the reward for a lifetime of hard labor . . . Efforts were made to counteract the principle that work had value in itself, arguing that the psychological and social needs met in the workplace could be fulfilled just as well outside of it . . .

On August 3, 1962, the cover story of *Time* magazine featured the rapid aging of Americans who had lots of time and money but no place in society . . . The article talked about how Del Webb's Sun City and similar age-segregated housing developments that focused on leisure in Arizona and elsewhere were transforming America's image of retirement into a time of self-absorption and fun . . . The results were stunning. In 1951, among men receiving Social Security benefits, 3 percent retired from work to pursue leisure; in 1963, 17 percent indicated that leisure was the primary reason for retiring from work; and by 1982, nearly 50 percent of men said they were retiring to pursue leisure.

While there were positive results for some older adults who took this path, it also led many into self-absorption and prejudice, tensions with younger people, boredom, and lack of a sense that they were contributing to society and to others' lives.

Let's remember three things:

Retirement is a new concept. It didn't exist before the twentieth century anywhere in the world except Germany. It didn't exist before the nineteenth century anywhere.

Retirement is a Western concept. It doesn't exist in Okinawa or much of the developing world. Old people in those places don't play golf every day. They contribute to their families and societies.

Retirement is a broken concept. It is based on three assumptions that aren't true: that we enjoy doing nothing instead of being productive, that we can afford to live well while earning no money for decades, and that we can afford to pay others to earn no money for decades.

6

"When you're through changing, you're through."

Willliam Safire was a speechwriter for President Nixon and a Pulitzer Prize–winning columnist for *The New York Times* who wrote for the newspaper for thirty-two years. After the first twenty-eight years writing an Op-Ed column twice a week *plus* a famous Sunday column on the English language, he decided to turn things down a notch in 2005 at the ripe age of seventy-five years old.

At ten years older than "retirement age," Bill didn't just retire, though. He kept writing the Sunday language column every week (just ditching the Op-Eds) and took on a new job as chairman of the Dana Foundation for four more years until his eventual death of pancreatic cancer in 2009.

Quite a run.

But what I want to tell you about is that famous day of January 24, 2005, when Bill Safire quit writing his famous twice-weekly Op-Eds. People were disappointed! It was the end of a voice. But how did he mark the finish of his famous column? He wrote an Op-Ed about it, of course. It was called "Never Retire." Here are some excerpts:

> The Nobel laureate James Watson, who started a revolution in science as co-discoverer of the structure of DNA, put it to me straight a couple of years ago: "Never retire. Your brain needs exercise or it will atrophy."

Why, then, am I bidding Op-Ed readers farewell today after more than 3,000 columns? Nobody pushed me; at 75, I'm in good shape, not afflicted with political ennui; and my recent column about tsunami injustice and the Book of Job drew the biggest mail response in 32 years of pounding out punditry.

Here's why I'm outta here: In an interview 50 years before, the aging adman Bruce Barton told me something like Watson's advice about the need to keep trying something new, which I punched up into "When you're through changing, you're through." He gladly adopted the aphorism, which I've been attributing to him ever since.

Combine those two bits of counsel—never retire, but plan to change your career to keep your synapses snapping—and you can see the path I'm now taking. Readers, too, may want to think about a longevity strategy.

We're all living longer. In the past century, life expectancy for Americans has risen from 47 to 77. With cures for cancer, heart disease and stroke on the way, with genetic engineering, stem cell regeneration and organ transplants a certainty, the boomer generation will be averting illness, patching itself up and pushing well past the biblical limits of "threescore and ten."

But to what purpose? If the body sticks around while the brain wanders off, a longer lifetime becomes a burden on self and society. Extending the life of the body gains most meaning when we preserve the life of the mind . . .

But retraining and fresh stimulation are what all of us should require in "the last of life, for which the first was made." Athletes and dancers deal with the need to retrain in their 30's, workers in their 40's, managers in their 50's, politicians in their 60's, academics and media biggies in their 70's. The trick is to start early in our careers the stress-relieving avocation that we will need later as a mind-exercising final vocation. We can quit a job, but we quit fresh involvement at our mental peril.

In this inaugural winter of 2005, the government in Washington is dividing with partisan zeal over the need or the way to protect today's 20-somethings' Social Security accounts in 2040. Sooner or later, we'll bite that bullet; personal economic security is freedom from fear.

But how many of us are planning now for our social activity accounts? Intellectual renewal is not a vast new government program, and to secure continuing social interaction deepens no deficit. By laying the basis for future activities in the midst of current careers, we reject stultifying retirement and seize the opportunity for an exhilarating second wind.

Medical and genetic science will surely stretch our life spans. Neuroscience will just as certainly make possible the mental agility of the aging. Nobody should fail to capitalize on the physical and mental gifts to come.

When you're through changing, learning, working to stay involved—only then are you through.

Work gives us so much—free and simple gifts we are given every day. These gifts are worth much more than any numbers on a paycheck, because they help us live truly rich lives. The freedom you feel from a satisfying job beats the oppressing ache of emptiness any day.

7
The 4 *S*'s of work

Why work?
Let's break it down.

Social

Let's flash back 1.2 million years. Before the Internet, before computers, before TVs, before you, before newspapers, before your parents, before cars, before your grandparents, before buildings, before your great-grandparents, before cities, before bikes, before lights, before clothes, before jewelry, before music, before art, before talking, before marriage, before fire, before weapons, before everything we know.

The Earth was here and it was empty. Trees, water, and dirt.

And then suddenly we appeared on the African plains. But, to be honest, it didn't look like we would last very long. After all, we couldn't fly, we couldn't swim, we didn't have claws, we didn't have big teeth, we couldn't see in the dark, we couldn't run faster than a rhino, we couldn't beat up a chimpanzee. We didn't seem to have much going for us. It looked like we would be lunch meat for giant leopards and saber-toothed tigers with dagger claws and twelve-inch-long curved teeth.

Yet flash-forward 1.2 million years and we're the most dominant mammal on the planet and many of the other animals around back then are now extinct.

See, we had a secret. And it was hidden between our ears. The human brain is the most complicated object in the entire universe. And it helped us take over the planet.

Over the past 1.2 million years the size of our brains has doubled and we have grown our population to more than seven billion from only a few scattered hundreds.

It was with these brains that we discovered leaving empty ostrich eggs out when it rained and stabbing hollow sticks of grass into the ground allowed us to collect water when there was a drought. It was with these brains that we first developed tools such as hunting spears and daggers to help us kill animals so we could eat. It was with these brains that we first developed language and the ability to communicate with one another. These brains started living in tribes and relying on one another in communities. These brains developed empathy and the desire to take care of other people in the tribe so they would take care of us, too.

Our brains were the foundation of our development as the most social species on the planet. Because, to put it simply, if you weren't social back then . . . *you died.*

Today study after study shows that it is our social connections that are *the single biggest driver of our happiness.*

New York Times—bestselling author Daniel Gilbert writes in *Stumbling on Happiness*: "If I wanted to predict your happiness and I could only know one thing about you, I wouldn't want to know about your gender, religion, health, or income. I'd want to know about the strength of your relationships with your friends and family."

People always ask me: What do you mean you work at Walmart? Don't you spend all your time writing books and giving speeches?

No, no way. I tell them if I was sitting at home in a dark room in front of a bright screen all day, I'd go crazy! It would feel lonely. I'd miss the social interaction I get from work.

The number one reason why work is important is because it is social. It's what adds richness to our days.

Carpooling, mentor sessions, open work settings, team charity drives, conferences, listening groups, appreciation emails, Friday team breakfasts, starting the meeting with recognition, business book clubs, lunchtime running groups, networking dinners, going to the gym together, even figuring out meeting politics.

We need to be social to be happy. Work provides major social stimulation.

Structure

What do Warren Buffett, Jay Z, Barack Obama, Oprah Winfrey, Brad Pitt, Mark Zuckerberg, Bono, Ellen DeGeneres, the Dalai Lama, and Bill Gates all have in common?

Sure, they're famous, they're rich, but there's something else.

They all have 168 hours in their weeks. No more, no less.

The richest man in the world can't buy more time. It's just not for sale.

So the question isn't how can we create more time but how can we use our time more effectively? We can't acquire time. But we can *structure* our time so we can get more out of our lives.

Work provides this structure.

Let me show you what I mean.

First off, the beautiful thing about 168 hours is that it divides into three very easily:

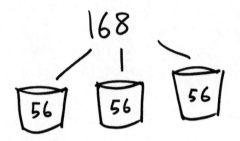

Congratulations! You have three fifty-six-hour buckets every single week.

Every Monday morning, every single person on Earth is given 168 hours and they have to spend every one of them by the strike of midnight on Sunday. Because time is something we made up, something we placed over the chaos of life to organize our lives, something that is free, easy, and always there . . . we don't feel the pain of wasting it.

I like sleeping eight hours a night. I can't always pull it off! But doctors and research keep saying it's so good for you. Unless you're taking care of a newborn, most people choose what time they go to bed. Not what time to get up . . . but what time you get down. So what's seven nights of eight-hour sleep cost?

You got it.

One whole fifty-six-hour bucket.

Me, I also work a full-time job at Walmart. Even though I'm scheduled to do that for forty hours each week, the truth is I include my drive to and from the office as work, too. I'm thinking about work, I'm going to work, I might be on the phone with someone about work. I'm working! And there are times I'm at home that I'm emailing a coworker, emailing my boss, or occasionally doing other work at night. In total, you know how many hours my job costs me?

You got it.

Another whole bucket.

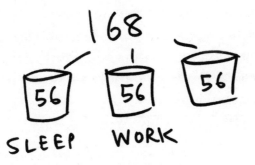

This scribble is similar for most working people. A bucket of sleep. A bucket of work. But here's the big breakthrough: You have an entire fifty-six-hour bucket left! And if you sleep or work less than fifty-six hours, congrats! Your third bucket is even bigger than mine.

This is your third bucket.

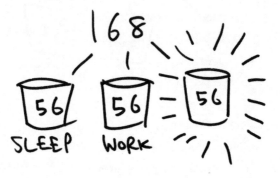

You have a big third bucket every week! It's your going-out-for-dinner bucket. Your spending-time-with-friends bucket. This is the bucket where you watch movies with your kids, play in your soccer league, go for jogs and lift weights, phone friends or call home, coach your kid's baseball team, write in coffee shops, listen to music, stay out late, and make love.

Our work bucket earns us our third bucket.

By structuring our time so that we're focused and investing our energy in a productive way, we earn and justify all the fun we have in our third bucket.

Work provides this structure!

Work *pays* for this structure.

When the Monday to Friday, nine-to-five lines disappear from our weeks, our lives get blurry. You always feel the drain of wanting to work. You need money. You need social stimulation. And you always want to balance this by spending time with family, friends, and kids.

Think about how you want to spend your third bucket every week.

For me, for nearly the past ten years of my life I've spent my third bucket writing 1000awesomethings.com, writing *The Book of Awesome* and its sequels, doing speeches and workshops, founding the Institute for Global Happiness, and developing the ideas on living a happy life that fill this book you're reading. While trying to spend my time living them!

It cost me an entire bucket for ten years.

But my point is you need to spend your third bucket on your passion. You deserve to spend that third bucket on your passion. Know what you're spending your third bucket on.

And make sure it's something you love.

Stimulation

I love hanging out with three-year-olds. I love the way they see the world, because they're seeing the world for the first time. A three-year-old can stare at a bug crossing the sidewalk for half an hour. Three-year-olds drop their jaws at their first baseball game—soaking in the crack of the bat, the roar of the crowd, the smell of the popcorn. A three-year-old can spend an entire afternoon picking dandelions in the backyard just to drop them into a glass of water as the centerpiece for dinner.

Having a sense of stimulation is about embracing your inner three-year-old!

Every day at work, you experience hundreds of tiny joys. They're easy to overlook. But work exposes us to simple joys every day.

When everyone nods at the thing you just said in the meeting. The guy who fixes the photocopier for you. Coming back from lunch to a way better parking spot. When the meeting ends early.

A coworker showing you a keyboard shortcut on your computer. Leftover cake in the office kitchen. The feeling you get after finishing a big project right at the deadline and knowing you did a great job. When someone decorates your cubicle for your birthday.

When I speak to companies I ask everybody in the audience to spend thirty seconds writing down one awesome thing that happens to them at work. We leave cue cards on their chairs beforehand. Then I ask people to trade their cue card with somebody who they've never talked to before. And then we read the cue cards in front of the room. That's when we realize that in a span of seconds we came up with thousands of awesome things together.

"When there's hot water left in the kettle so I don't have to heat any up."

"When the person you're meeting is even later than you are."

"When the boss says thank you."

The point is that work gives us a place to learn and discover so many new things about our lives and our world. We don't hire our coworkers! So there are diverse ages, backgrounds, experiences, and thoughts that we don't always get from friends and family.

Retiring slices off this learning, seeing, and experiencing the stimulation of our world.

Story

The pacemaker was invented in 1899 when J. A. MacWilliam reported in the *British Medical Journal* the discovery that an electric impulse to the human heart causes a "ventricular contraction"—in other words, you could make a heart beat by zapping it with power! In the 1920s an early version of the pacemaker appeared. It plugged in to your heart . . . and plugged into the wall. Which was great! Except that when the power went out . . . so did you. Still, they used this early version to revive a stillborn infant in 1928 in Sydney, Australia. After ten minutes the baby's heart beat of its own accord. Suddenly, there was potential. Between the 1930s and World War II pacemaker development went silent. No improvements, no new technologies, no commercialization. Why? They became taboo. People thought pacemakers "revived the dead" and didn't like the idea of tampering with nature. Must have seen too many zombie movies. Eventually, in the 1960s, fully implantable pacemakers were popularized by a company called Medtronic.

Why do I tell you all this? Because Medtronic has a great story. What's their mission? What's their story? What are they trying to do? Here's an edited version:

> To contribute to human welfare by alleviating pain, restoring health, and extending life.

Impressive. Beautiful. A great story. If you work at Medtronic, you can probably get behind that. "I help extend life and restore health." And they make it easy to get behind it, too. The company brings its story to life by printing it on walls throughout the office and having patients read how Medtronic devices touched their lives at big company meetings. Can you imagine how you would feel if an eleven-year-old girl got on stage to read a letter, saying, "Thank you for giving my dad eight extra years to live after his heart attack. I got to take photos and make memories that I wouldn't have otherwise had"?

I bet the story of your company would really resonate with you. Every company has a story!

Coke wants to give the world happiness breaks. Harvard Business School is educating leaders who make a difference in the world. Facebook is making the world more connected. Wikipedia is giving the sum of human knowledge to every single person for free. The Red Cross prevents and alleviates human pain and suffering. Google is organizing the world's information.

Story.

When you're working you become part of something bigger than yourself. Volunteer at the library and you spread knowledge to the community. Teach at the college and you're developing productive members of society. Write for the city's biggest blog and you're creating community.

What does retiring do?

It chops you out of a productive story. You aren't part of something bigger than yourself anymore. This hampers your ikigai!

So don't give up work. You'll be giving up the Social, Structure, Stimulation, and Story you get every day from being there.

Forget the money.

You'll lose the 4 S's, and they are much more important.

8

The dream we all have
that is completely wrong

I will never get the chance to ask him about it, but I'm sure the saddest I saw Mr. Wilson was on those final few weeks before he retired. He didn't want to go. He loved the students, he loved the school, he loved helping kids navigate their paths in life.

The government forced him to give up the thing he wanted most. They took away Monday-morning coffees with the guidance office secretaries, hallway walks at lunch, and the energy from a thousand teenagers every day. They took away his sense of helping kids through family troubles, failing grades, and anxiety about decisions. They took away the things he loved the most.

Mr. Wilson taught me that retirement, as we think of it today, isn't a dream we actually want. We don't actually want to do nothing. We just want to do something we love.

Hazel McCallion was ninety-three years old when she decided she would retire from being mayor of Mississauga, Ontario, Canada's fifth-largest city. That's after she held the job for more than forty straight years, winning twelve straight elections, and outlasting *eight* Canadian prime ministers.

Why did she keep going nearly thirty years after "retirement age"?

"There are still challenges," she said. "I don't know what I'd do. And I want to keep busy."

We want challenges. Challenges let us contribute a sense of giving, learning, and improving to ourselves and the world. We feel alive. We experience life. We feel like we can do anything.

According to *Merriam-Webster,* retirement means "withdrawal from one's position or occupation or from active working life." In other words, dropping out and going home. Dropping your withered bones off at the beach. What happens when you withdraw from active working life? You idle, which is defined as "to spend time doing nothing." What happens when you do nothing? You get bored.

According to *Merriam-Webster,* boredom is "the state of being weary and restless through lack of interest."

Feeling weary because one is unoccupied.

Is that what you want?

Indonesian author Toba Beta says, "You get old faster when you think about retirement."

So what's the dream we all have that is completely wrong?

Retirement.

Fortune magazine published a report saying the two most dangerous years of our lives are the year we're born . . . and the year we retire.

There's a reason retirement killed my favorite guidance counselor.

Because *we give away* our ikigai and we do it to ourselves, with planning, with purpose.

Together with the sudden loss of Social, Structure, Stimulation, and Story, what we find in the barren tundra of retirement is the cold, wet, guilt-drenched thought that *this* is what we wanted, *this* is what we worked our whole lives toward, *this* is the pot of gold at the end of the rainbow.

But there is no pot of gold.

Remember the 4 *S*'s when you're lost.

The world has far more problems, opportunities, and challenges than it has people like you to do interesting and meaningful work on them. There is so much you can do. There are so many places to go. I know when you look you'll always find meaty projects and passionate causes you can sink your teeth into.

Just keep learning, keep changing, and keeping growing.

And promise me that you will never retire.

BE HAPPY FIRST

DO IT FOR YOU

REMEMBER THE LOTTERY

NEVER RETIRE

Secret #5

How to Make

More Money Than

a Harvard MBA

1
What does Harvard do for your salary?

Harvard makes you feel rich.

I walked through campus for two years feeling like I'd been cast as Moneybags in a movie about ruling the world and having it all.

On Harvard's campus, tall twisting oak trees blow softly in the wind, casting polka-dot shadows over beautiful red-brick buildings, manicured ivy, and rolling lawns. Students ease open thirty-foot-tall carved wooden doors before stepping into marble-tiled libraries. Between classes, students grab made-to-order sushi from the cafeteria before eating with friends on brown leather couches against walls covered with expensive original art.

The students at Harvard Business School feel rich because they either are rich . . . or they're about to get rich.

The average graduating salary is $120,000!

To put that in perspective, the average American makes $24,000.

$$\frac{\$120,000}{\$24,000} = 5$$

That means a fresh-faced, dewy-eyed twenty-six-year-old with two years of business school under his or her belt makes five times what the average American citizen makes. I know my salary almost tripled after I graduated from Harvard. Yes, Harvard makes you feel rich because it actually makes you rich.

Or does it?

2
"Is everyone nuts?"

was sad when I graduated, because all my friends were scattering in different directions. After a big road trip, it was suddenly all over and then:

Mark and his wife moved to Houston, and he got a job with a high-end consulting company. About a quarter of Harvard Business School grads go work for consulting firms, and the hours are notoriously tough. Unless they land a local assignment, most consultants fly out Monday mornings and fly home Thursday nights, every single week, every single month, forever.

Chris went to Washington, DC, to be assistant principal at a big charter school. We kept in touch, but he was always at work when I called. We talked about our road trip and I'd ask him, "Are you getting any sleep these days?" He'd say, "Well, I get to work every morning around 7:00 a.m. and get home around 9:00 p.m. I usually go in for a few hours on the weekend, too. So yeah, enough sleep, but not much else."

Ryan went into private equity in New York. Another quarter of Harvard Business School grads get high-end finance jobs in investment banking, private equity, or hedge funds. They help big companies buy each other, invest in illiquid assets, create complicated investments. But Ryan told me he started work around 10:00 a.m. and worked till 11:00 p.m., seven days a week.

Sonia went to work in Silicon Valley at a big tech company. The tech giants hired nearly another quarter of the graduates from our class and had great reputations for gourmet meals, dry-cleaning, and Ping-Pong tables at the office. When I reached out to Sonia a year after graduation she told me she loved her job and was working about eighty hours a week.

It seemed crazy to me, but all my friends were working eighty to one hundred hours a week.

And a week only has 168 hours in it!

Where was their third bucket?

I remember thinking, Is everyone nuts?

I thought back to Harvard and remembered going out for dinner with a group of McKinsey consultants during a recruiting event. They flew to Boston and wined and dined us at a ritzy joint. We drank expensive wines, ate delicious food, and talked about world issues into the wee hours. My brain was overheating because of the stimulating conversation. These guys were warm, friendly, and killer smart. It was a great night.

But the thing I remember most is that when we were finally finishing up around two in the morning, all the McKinsey consultants were . . . going back to work! They were jumping on conference calls with teams in Shanghai, opening laptops to do emails, or getting together to finalize presentations for the next day. At two in the morning!

Consultants and finance folks make up most of Harvard Business School grads and they work approximately eighty to one hundred hours a week.

So, are they really making $120,000 a year?

3

The single calculation to find out what you *really* make

D o you remember fractions? I learned them back in fourth grade in a moldy classroom with flickering florescent lights in my elementary school. Pink chalk dust scrawled across blackboards showing us how one-half can be written as ½ or three-quarters can be written as ¾ . . . with *3* being the **numerator** and *4* being the **denominator**. As in "I sat on the couch in sweatpants watching TV all Saturday night and ate ¾ of a pepperoni pizza."

Well, the Harvard salary of $120,000 is a fraction, too.

It means you make:

$$\frac{\$\,120,000 \ \text{dollars}}{1 \ \text{year of work}}$$

That sounds great, but there's one little problem with that fraction. Nobody works every single hour of the year. Therefore, it doesn't make sense talking about how much money you make *over an entire year of work*. That makes salaries sound like giant cardboard paychecks handed out on New Year's Eve with hearty handshakes. "Congrats, Sampson. You blew away your sales numbers for the past twelve months. After a solid year of grinding it out every single day, you have finally earned this—your annual paycheck."

But it doesn't work that way.

We don't earn big fat dollars for years of work.

We earn tiny little dollars for hours of work.

When I had my first babysitting job I worked for $5/hour. Pretty sweet deal for watching *Alf* with a couple of eight-year-olds while eating unlimited cheese strings. Then I did yardwork for my parents for $10/hour. That was generous of them, since the going rate for raking leaves and shoveling driveways was lower than that. Although I did help them avoid pesky health insurance by getting paid under the table. Some of my friends did construction for $12/hour. Some lifeguarded at pools for $16/hour. Point is: Every single job is paid by the hour. Some are forty hours a week, some are eighty, some are one hundred and twenty. But no matter how much money you're making, the numerator is how much you get and the denominator is how much you work.

Every single job is paid by the hour.

Harvard Business School grads make double or triple the money a lot of people make, but they often work double or triple the hours, too. When you work that much, it's harder to find time to shovel the driveway, play with your kids, or plant your garden, so maybe you hire people on the cheap to do those things for you. You will still have fun! Frankly, the money you're making can afford luxury vacations and expensive restaurants. You may have even more fun. But there's less time for fun. Your third bucket disappears.

Think about whether it's important to you to feel the pride of a freshly shoveled driveway, the joy of watching your kids discover a new word, or see the tulips you planted in the fall finally bloom in the spring.

There's nothing wrong with either life.

But think about the life you want.

4

How does a teacher
or retail assistant manager
make more than a Harvard MBA?

Time for a scribble.

Here's how much a Harvard MBA makes compared to two very common jobs: an assistant manager at a retail store and an elementary school teacher.

		Harvard MBA	Retail Asst. Mgr.	Teacher
(A)	Salary/year	$120,000	$70,000	$45,000
(B)	Vacation	2 weeks	2 weeks	12 weeks
(C) (A-B)	Weeks working/year	50 weeks	50 weeks	40 weeks
(D)	Hours/week	85	50	40
(E) (C×D)	Hours/year	4250	2500	1600
(F)	Salary/hour	$28	$28	$28

They all make $28/hour.

Where did I get the numbers from?

Well, teachers are scheduled for seven-hour school days (usually 8:30 a.m. to 3:30 p.m.) with typically an hour off for lunch. Let's round that up to thirty working hours a week. But we all know how hard teachers work. We know it's way more than that! My dad is a teacher, my wife Leslie is a teacher, and they bring work home. The average teacher does an hour or two of work every single night! Marking, prepping, coaching a team. So I added ten hours a week for that.

Retail store assistant managers are typically scheduled for forty-hour workweeks, but it's a tough job. They end up working before or after shifts sometimes. There are questions, issues pop up, people call them at home. So I added ten hours a week for that.

And the eighty-five hours for Harvard MBAs? It's a ballpark average figure based on my data, research, and personal experience. Working on consulting gigs in a Chicago hotel room or slaving away on an investment banking deal doesn't exactly give you free evenings or weekends.

Although these numbers are generally accurate, of course there are exceptions—maybe you're a teacher who works eighty-five hours a week or a Harvard MBA who works forty. But stick with me here, because this secret still has meaning for you.

What's the bottom line?

They all make $28/hour!

So how do you make more money than a Harvard MBA?

Two ways:

1. Work more hours *and* make way more per year.
2. Work way less hours *and* make less per year.

This works because when you overvalue your time you make **more** money by working less hours and earning more dollars *per* hour.

But wait: Am I telling you to work less? Absolutely not! My point isn't that you should suddenly dial down your interests, passion, or career. My point is to calculate how much you make *per hour* and know this number. Remember this number. Have this number in your head. I have friends who work around the clock as downtown lawyers and they joke, "When I do the math I actually make less than minimum wage." They're right! And, frankly, I don't understand them.

Do not make less than minimum wage.

The way to make more money than a Harvard MBA isn't to get your annual salary over $120,000 or $150,000 or $500,000. It's to measure how much you make per hour and **overvalue you** so you're spending time working only on things you enjoy. The average life expectancy in our world today is seventy years, and we sleep for a third of that. That means you have four hundred thousand waking hours in your life total. You have four hundred thousand hours to spend in your life total.

Understand how much a Harvard MBA really makes and **overvalue you** so every single hour of your working life is spent doing something you love.

BE HAPPY FIRST

DO IT FOR YOU

REMEMBER THE LOTTERY

NEVER RETIRE

OVERVALUE YOU

Secret #6

The Secret to

Never Being

Too Busy Again

1

Do this and you'll suddenly have space back in your life

For years, I've watched many business leaders burn out. Sometimes flame out spectacularly. Consultants traveling for months suddenly have anxiety attacks on airplanes. High-powered CEOs in their forties having heart attacks or strokes. Suicide attempts. I don't want to scare you, but leaders doing too much are bubbling with fire inside—and not the good kind.

Here's another scribble. This one's called the Space Scribble, and it reflects what I have learned from those leaders who have been able to manage *high doing* and *high thinking*. Instead of checking themselves into hospitals, they knew how to surf between waves of thinking and doing with skill. I've seen the Space Scribble mastered by a CEO of a hospitality company, a multibillionaire luxury goods merchant, and a three-time *New York Times*–bestselling author. No, it doesn't take a specific personality, makeup, or mood. You just have to want balance.

The Space Scribble helps you get more done *and* be happier doing it. It's good news for your future bosses, lovers, and kids.

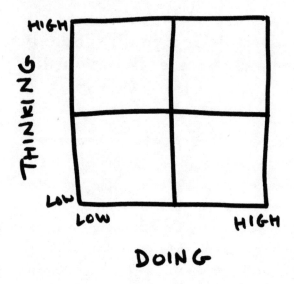

In the top right corner of this scribble is doing, doing, doing, thinking, thinking, thinking. When we're going really hard, we're all right there. Highest possible thinking! Highest possible doing! Up all night prepping for a conference. Week of the big launch. First month on the job. It feels great to be in that corner.

You're in the moment. You're in the zone. You're burning.

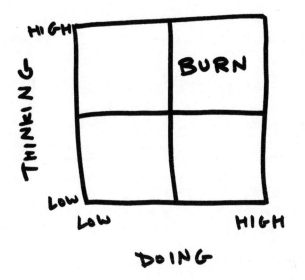

Yes, if you're doing a lot and thinking a lot, you're burning at both ends. Which two ends? Your thinking end and your doing end.

Take it from Pulitzer Prize–winning poet Edna St. Vincent Millay in her book *Poetry*, published in June 1918:

> *My candle burns at both ends;*
> *It will not last the night;*
> *But ah, my foes, and oh, my friends—*
> *It gives a lovely light!*

Burn gives a lovely light. Yes, it's hard to leave the Burn box because you're getting so much done. You're incredibly productive! It's a massive high. Adrenaline squeezed from battery-size glands on top of your kidneys keeps you turbocharged. And beware of feedback mechanisms. They often can't be trusted. A big bonus rewards extra efforts. Customers send thank-you notes for bending over backward. Your boss congratulates you on hitting an aggressive deadline . . . and then presents an even more aggressive one. Is this feedback malicious? It's not meant to be! But it's a dangerous side effect of finding a business model that works.

A senior partner at a prestigious global consulting firm once said to me after a boozy dinner, "We find type A superachievers from Ivy League schools who need lots of rewards and praise . . . and then dangle carrots just over the next deadline, project, and promotion, so they keep pushing themselves. Over every hill is an even bigger reward . . . and an even bigger hill."

The Burn is so seductive because it's so productive.

You feel great there.

Is it any wonder I once heard a retail COO say on a conference panel, "It's a bad sign when a store manager buys a house. Means they're settling down. Means they might get stale. We move the best managers from city to city to city so they have a new community to learn and new social and work systems to develop. It gives the stores great energy to have new ideas. And when they get comfortable, we move them again!" He didn't say this at the head of a mahogany table while petting a cat and filling a room with evil laughter. He just shared what worked best for his business. It was his job to do what was best.

My point is that there's nothing wrong with burning. But there is something wrong with burning *out*. It feels great to get a lot done, but just be careful you don't go too hard, too long. That's when you slip right off the edge of the scribble. Very few people have the courage to tell you that you're near your max. Nervous breakdowns, tearful breakups, and heart attacks always come far too late.

So what's the solution?

You must create space.

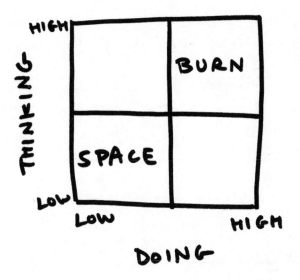

Space is the exact opposite of Burn.

No thinking, no doing. This is the sandy beach vacation without plans, phones, or thoughts. Lying on a beach chair while sunbeams soak you, waves pound in the distance, and your mind slowly lets go of everything it's silently squeezing. That's space. It's not the vacation with the packed itinerary or your email buzzing in the background. Those don't turn off the doing and thinking parts of your brain. Wooded cabins, meditative retreats, or locking yourself in the bathroom can also give you space. You need space! But let me caution that, just like Burn, the Space box can be toxic in high doses.

What do I mean?

My mom retired from her government job at the same time my sister and I moved out of the house while my dad was still motoring around town every day. She was suddenly home alone without social structure, planned activities, or a group of friends. She was in a great thinking phase for a while, but eventually she noticed her weekdays and weekends blurring together, personal problems becoming unproductive, and simply not having enough to do or think about. This continued until she joined a bridge club and a professional network and had a granddaughter to care for one day a week. Space without an end date—or an ikigai—can lead to swirling and swirling.

What happens in the other two boxes?

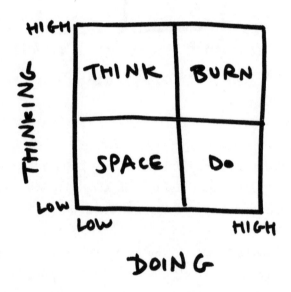

Think means you're thinking. Pretty simple. You're reflecting, spacing yourself from doing anything, but still engaging your mind. Journaling. Writing a book. Talking about an issue at work with a friend, partner, or therapist. All great things to do. All physically relaxing, which allows you to completely indulge and engage in your thoughts.

Do means you're doing. No thinking! Just doing. Hiking a mountain. Working out intensely. Physically engaged. All your blood pounds to your muscles and lets your mind slip away and relax.

The Space Scribble says every single moment you're in one of four boxes.

And every single moment you need to know which one you're in and which you're going to next.

Happy people alternate between boxes. They flip-flop. They swirl. They jump. They know where they are and they know how to create space.

2

The 3 *B*'s of creating space

Does creating space just mean taking a break? Doing nothing? No, it's much more important than that.

The space itself has productive purpose.

Chris Ulrich is the head of a growing tech company. Digital apps, digital currency, digital development—his entire life is digital. But he says his best ideas come from the notepad he leaves beside his bed. A former retail CEO told me his biggest business problems were always solved by a long jog in the woods. Imagine! Not the office, boardroom, or conferences. Just running in the woods. And Teddy Kravitz, who runs one of North America's largest talent agencies, says he can't explain it, but whenever he's on his three-hour Sunday-morning bike ride he always gets a brilliant idea how he can do something differently. He says he's rigged up his cell phone on his arm to leave voicemails to himself while riding.

Creativity researchers sometimes refer to places ideas suddenly pop into our heads as the three *B*'s:

BED
BATHTUB
BUS

"When we take time off from working on a problem, we change what we're doing and our context, and that activates different areas of our brain," says Keith Sawyer, author of *Explaining Creativity*. "If the answer wasn't in the part of the brain we were using, it might be in another. If we're lucky, in the next context we may hear or see something that relates—distantly—to the problem we had temporarily put aside."

Where did Newton discover gravity? Sitting under an apple tree.

Where did Niels Bohr discover the structure of the atom? In a lab with gigantic microscopes? In a classroom with walls of equations on blackboards? During a meeting with the world's greatest minds? No, he was led by strange images in his dreams.

Where did Archimedes discover that the volume of irregular objects could be measured by water displacement? This was two thousand years ago in Ancient Greece, mind you. Surely he must have met with kings, studied ideas from Plato, or debated scientific insights in lengthy letters with contemporaries? No, he was stepping into a bath and noticed the water spill over the tub. When he made the connection he shouted, "Eureka!" which is Ancient Greek for "I have found it!"

3

This is how NASA, Alfred Hitchcock, and Nicole Katsuras use this secret

W hy does creating space work?

Stop thinking to do. Stop doing to think. Stop both and your brain gets really excited.

Trouble struck NASA in 1993 when their revolutionary Hubble Space Telescope broke down. There it was, spinning around Earth, way up in the sky, with a busted ninety-six-inch mirror—unable to do the thing it was blasted up there to do, which was take pictures of the universe to figure out how big and old our starry home is. Pretty important job.

NASA was reeling from the *Challenger* disaster of 1986 and completely losing a *Mars Observer* the year before. Whoops! Those only cost 813 million dollars. Now their telescope was flying around broken. They were a laughingstock. They were stressed. "We all feel extra pressure," Joseph Rothenberg, NASA's associate director of flight projects, said at the time. What if funding was cut? Programs chopped? So they did what many organizations do when they're scared and in trouble: Double down. Bet it all. Go for broke.

NASA opened the purse strings and spent a year training their most experienced astronauts with two hundred custom-made tools to go up and actually try to fix the distorted mirror inside the Hubble Space Telescope *while it flew around outer space.* They had to save their reputation.

But there was just one problem.

As the months went on, as scientists burned cash, nobody could figure out how they were actually going to attach this new mirror inside the telescope.

Where did the solution eventually come from?

Creating space.

One day NASA engineer Jim Crocker was taking a shower in a hotel in Germany and he noticed the European-style showerhead mounted on adjustable rods with folding arms. A brain wave occurred, and Jim pictured using the same rods to mount the new mirrors inside the Hubble.

Flash-forward and this moment of clarity was the secret to fixing the telescope and allowing it to function to this day. Jim wasn't working late on Friday. He wasn't in the lab all weekend. He was in the shower on vacation, allowing his brain the space to relax. When it wasn't told what to do, it did its own thing. Today the Hubble routinely pulls back colorful, mind-bending images that expand imaginations around the world. All from a German shower.

Alfred Hitchcock is called the Master of Suspense and directed more than fifty films over six decades, including *Psycho* and *The Birds.* How did he create space while working on a tough screenplay?

One of his cowriters says: "When we came up against a block and our discussions became very heated and intense, he would stop suddenly and tell a story that had nothing to do with the work at hand. At first I was almost outraged and then I discovered that he did this intentionally. He mistrusted working under pressure, and he would say, 'We're pressing, we're pressing, we're working too hard. Relax, it will come.' And of course it finally always did."

Creating space in our minds allows thoughts to swish and swirl around without us stirring them with a wooden spoon. They are free. They fly in different directions. And we often like the taste of what comes back.

Creating space even works in less obvious ways. Take abstract painter Nicole Katsuras, whose work is exhibited in London, Seoul, and Paris. Stephen Ranger, a contemporary art specialist at Waddington's, describes her work as "quasi-abstractions that transcend the inherent limits of pictures, sharing a vision that is uniquely hers."

What does Nicole Katsuras say about creating space?

"I find my most creative period in the studio is when I reach a space that I call the void. That's when time slows down and speeds up all at once. My unconscious and conscious are calm and I am no longer aware. When I reach the void, I am totally consumed with pushing paint on canvas. A sort of meditative state. Around me is just white noise—a humming of nothing—devoid of thought, sound, and everything physical, other than my paint and canvas. In the void I never remember how much time has passed or what I was doing before or during. It is my most productive creative time. It is where some of my best work happens."

What about the actual white space she has in her paintings?

"I try to re-create these moments—little plateaus, breaks, and resting spots amongst the abstract imagery for the viewer's eyes to rest from the organized chaos of thick, colorful, sculptural gobs of paint. I think that moments of stillness are important to appreciate both the big and small things that are all around us."

So how do you create space?

How do you free your mind like Newton, Bohr, or Archimedes? How do you open your brain to receive insights worthy of NASA, Hitchcock, or Katsuras? How do you clear your thoughts so you have space to come up with innovative ideas that challenge your business? Is it as simple as jogging on Sunday mornings?

No. It's not. You might not have time for that jog. You could be weighed down mentally while racing down the street. You may have too much going on. Big meetings, busy days.

You know the Space Scribble. You know you need to get there. But rather than just saying "Go on vacation more, dummy!" I want to share three *specific* and *tangible* ways you can create space.

I want to introduce the 3 Removals. Think of them as caped crusaders in menacing black masks holding big, sharp scythes. Ready to hack parts of your life away so you're free to do other things. Space comes from hacking. Space in dense jungles comes from hacking at vines. Space in calendars comes from hacking at meetings. Space in your life comes from hacking at choice, time, and access.

4

Removal #1: How to make every decision at twice the speed

We duck out of the tiny six-seat plane and step carefully down the metal stairs. Deep blue skies hang like wallpaper over the world as we stare at empty yellow fields all around us. I am the official tour guide for Peter Aston, a European clothing chain CEO, on a trip over the ocean visiting big-box discount stores. We are three days into flights over Great Lakes, jagged rocks, and thick boreal forests.

Fifteen minutes later we get out of a cab, walk into a store, and start walking around. He asks questions and takes photos and I make notes and follow-ups for him. We are walking around the store when we get to the clothing section and Peter suddenly stops. He looks stunned. Eyes popping open, he reaches for his phone and starts snapping pictures. He is excited. "Look how busy the department is," he says. "Customers are swarming over this section more than the last few like this. Notice how the last two stores are struggling to offer clear choices—mixed styles, colors smeared across the rainbow, inconsistent brands and labels. They were treasure hunts."

I nod. Same chain but a different look. And much busier.

"This clothing department looks completely different. Somebody has taken the clothes shipped by the head office, ditched most of them, and created their own offering with a consistent style, theme, and colors. Shirts on one side, pants on the other, dresses at the back. All the same three colors. This is one of the best clothing departments I've seen. Beats a lot of stores they have overseas."

Back on the plane to see a couple new stores in another town, I ask Peter what was so exciting about the display.

"Customers get the opinion of a trusted source. Someone you trust has made picks so you don't have to. Nobody has time to wade through foggy seas of endless decisions. They give up. Or make bad choices. That display says here's the color, here's the style, here's what you want. Take it or leave it. There are less decisions so you feel confident and trust the opinion.

"Early in my career I worked a summer job helping a buyer for fish in an American supermarket chain," he continues. "We had every kind of fish. We had every kind of seasoning. It was all fresh. It was priced well. But nobody bought it. We couldn't figure it out. Finally we realized customers were scared of buying fresh fish. Which one tastes best? How do you season it? How do you cook it? Too many decisions. So we changed our section. We only carried three kinds of fish at a time. Not ten, not fifteen, three. And we had one kind of seasoning for each. So you suddenly only had one choice to make. Cajun trout, teriyaki salmon, or lemon sole? Once you made your pick, the fishmonger dipped your fish in the seasoning and the label printed off the instructions on how to cook it."

What happened?

"Sales were up over five hundred percent."

I realized fewer choices means faster decisions. Our brains don't need to mentally step into each new option and stretch out inside them, picturing them, evaluating them, holding them in our heads while we step into the next option.

Fewer choices means faster decisions.

How do the President of the United States and the CEO of Facebook make every decision at twice the speed?

Less time spent on decisions means more time for everything else.

What does President Obama tell us about making every decision at twice the speed? "You'll see I wear only gray or blue suits," he said in a 2012 *Vanity Fair* article. "I'm trying to pare down decisions. I don't want to make decisions about what I'm eating or wearing. Because I have too many other decisions to make. You need to focus your decision-making energy. You need to routinize yourself. You can't be going through the day distracted by trivia."

You can't be going through the day distracted by trivia.

What about Mark Zuckerberg, founder and CEO of Facebook?

"I own maybe twenty identical gray T-shirts. I mean, I wear the same thing every day, right?" he said in a *Today* interview.

Mark's not turning heads on the runway, but he doesn't care. His goal is building the world's largest social media company. A minute more a day picking a T-shirt is a minute less a day he's thinking about his company.

The curious case of Benjamin Lee

Cutting decisions, chopping decisions, cutting them out.

It takes me back to my first office job many years ago. I was twenty-two years old and had just graduated from university. Procter & Gamble hired me as assistant brand manager for Cover Girl and Max Factor makeup, and I started in the summer.

Benjamin Lee was the first person I met on my first day.

Chinese, in his midtwenties, Ben had thin, jumpy eyes, close-cropped hair, and wore tight dark clothes. I assumed he was a Zen

Master because his desk had no pictures, no artwork, and no office work on it—just a tiny bowl of rocks punctured with three bamboo shoots.

Ben's desk was right beside mine, and after a few weeks of working together I started noticing his style. Black shoes, black socks, black pants, brightly colored shirt. He looked good. Simple style. Everything fit.

"Can I ask you a question?" I asked him one night while working late. "Where do you get your clothes?"

He laughed. "You won't believe it. Once a year I buy thirty white boxers, thirty identical pairs of black socks, fifteen custom-fitted dress shirts, and five pairs of black pants. I do laundry once a month. I never match socks, I never shop on weekends, I never spend any time thinking about what I'm wearing. It's always the next thing in my closet. You'll probably see this blue shirt again in a couple weeks."

I thought back to a couple months prior, when I'd spent an entire Sunday shopping for what to wear on my first day at work. And a couple minutes every morning picking clothes. Laundry every weekend. And forget ever matching socks from the dryer.

"I calculated that never thinking about what to wear, doing laundry once a month, and going shopping once a year saves me fifteen minutes a day on average," Ben continued. "Maybe more because I don't lose any 'frictional time' jumping between thoughts. So I get eight to ten hours back every month. That's an extra week of waking hours each year. Do you know how much I can get done in an extra week?"

I knew how much Ben could get done in an extra week.

He was on the fast track, delivering results, well liked by peers and bosses. Although he worked long hours like everyone else, he wasn't working more hours than everyone else. He simply made better decisions, *by making fewer decisions*, by reserving his decision-making energy for things that mattered.

I had friends who spent time picking out cuff links, matching ties to socks, turning heads with trendy shirts. I know those friends wouldn't trade in time shopping for the world. Wasted time? No, they loved that time.

But for me, I started thinking about other things instead of thinking about what to wear.

How much time was I spending making decisions every day?

And which ones weren't important?

The most exhausting idea I've ever had

I decided to spend an entire day writing down every decision I made and then looking at which decisions I wanted to chop out of my life. Ben outsourced his clothing decisions! What could I outsource? This is the first step to understanding which decisions you can chop. An annoying process. But worth it. Here is every decision I made in one day:

Should I get up now or sleep a few more minutes?

Should I get up now or sleep a few more minutes?

Should I get up to go to the bathroom?

Should I have a glass of ice water or jump right in the shower?

Should I go to the gym?

Should I have a shower here or at the gym?

Do I have time to go to the gym before work if I leave now?

Should I eat breakfast after or make a shake for the car?

Should I put cinnamon in my shake?

Should I put yogurt in my shake?

Should I put spinach in my shake?

Should I put vitamin D in my shake?

Should I wear my work clothes to the gym and then change into my workout clothes there or wear my workout clothes to the gym and carry a hanger with all my work clothes on them?

What should I wear today?

Are these pants still clean?

Do these socks match this shirt?

Should I wear my brown belt or my black belt?

Which shirt should I wear?

Is this shirt too wrinkly?

Should I check email quickly now, in case there's anything urgent?

Should I respond to this email now or when I get to work?

What should I say to this email?

What should I say to *this* email?

Do I need a hat today?

Do I need a scarf today?

Should I wear brown shoes or black shoes?

Should I put my clothes in my trunk or in my front seat?

Should I listen to the radio or have quiet in the car?

Which station should I listen to?

Which route should I take to work today?

Should I listen for the traffic report in case there's an accident or just assume the highway is empty this time of the day?

Should I turn right on Queen Street or take Spadina to the Gardiner?

Should I try to pass this streetcar at the light or just stay behind it?

Should I turn left on Jameson to get to the highway or continue on Queen?

Should I turn left at Parkside to get to the highway or continue on Queen?

Should I gun it on this yellow light?

Should I turn left at Islington to get to the highway or continue on the Queensway?

Should I check email at this red light?

Should I check email at this red light?

Should I check email at this red light?

Should I turn left at Kipling to get to the highway or continue on the Queensway?

Should I check email at this red light?

Should I call Leslie to see if she woke up with her alarm clock?

Should I call anybody else?

Should I check my calendar for the day?

Should I park at the front door for convenience or far away to get extra exercise?

Should I change in this aisle or the aisle at the back of the locker room?

Should I take a full locker or a half-locker?

Do I need to lose weight around my stomach?

Do I need to shave today?

Do I look good?

Should I take a towel for my workout?

Should I do cardio or weights, or see if there's a class going on?

Should I warm up on the StairMaster, treadmill, elliptical, exercise bike, rowing machine, or step machine?

How long should I set the time for?

Should I enter my age and weight or try to skip this?

Should I pick Manual, Hill, Random, Fat Burn, Cardio, Interval Training, or Fitness Test?

Should I keep going past five minutes or stop and do weights?

Did I sweat on the machine enough to get paper towels and spray to clean it?

Should I start weights with free weights or with a machine?

Should I look up a workout on my phone or just wing it?

What exercise should I do?

Should I do squats on the rack or with dumbbells?

Should I do three sets or try for four sets?

Should I get water or keep going?

What exercise should I do now?

Is this bench inclined enough or should I set it back a notch or two?

How much weight should I use?

Should I warm up first?

Should I do three sets or try for four?

Should I get water or keep going?

What exercise should I do now?

Should I say hi to Jackie?

Does Jackie want to talk or is she in intense-workout mode?

Should I check my email?

What exercise should I do now?

Should I focus on my chest or try to make this a full-body workout?

Should I look up other chest exercises on my phone?

Should I do dips, Pec Deck, chest flies, bench press, incline bench press, or decline bench press?

Are there other chest exercises on another website that I'm forgetting?

Should I lay my towel on the bench or leave it to the side?

How much weight should I try?

Should I increase the weight?

Should I get water now or later?

Should I check my email?

Should I try for twelve reps or twenty reps?

Should I increase the weight?

Should I check my email?

Should I call it a workout or try to do another chest exercise?

Should I do dips, Pec Deck, bench press, incline bench press, or decline bench press?

How much weight should I do on Pec Deck?

Do I need to change this seat height?

Do I need to change this starting position for the handles?

Should I get water now?

Should I check my email?

Should I check my email?

Should I read this email?

Should I respond to this email?

What should I say to this email?

Should I do another exercise or finish off with abs?

Should I do planks or situps?

Should I do front plank or side plank or both?

How long should I try to go for?

Should I try to do that again or switch to side planks?

How long should I try to go for?

Do I need to clean my sweaty head print off the mat?

How should I clean up my sweaty head print off the mat?

Should I weigh myself?

Should I get a drink of water?

Should I check my email?

Should I get another towel for a bathmat on this locker room floor?

Should I leave my clothes here or lock them up while I shower?

Should I sit in the steam room or whirlpool before I shower?

Which shower has the best water pressure again?

Which hook should I leave my towel on?

Should I shampoo my hair?

Should I dry off here or outside the showers?

Should I spray that foot spray on my feet or forget it?

Should I fold my gym clothes or just stuff them in my bag?

Should I check the class schedule on my way out?

Should I have a protein shake?

Should I leave my protein shake container in the car or go wash it inside at work?

Should I try to find parking in the front lot or head straight to the back lot?

Should I check email now?

Do I have any dry cleaning to take in?

Should I check email now?

Should I get water and go to the bathroom or set up my computer?

Should I go say hi to my boss?

Should I check email now?

What should I focus my time on today?

Should I check email now?

Should I check voicemail now?

Should I answer this instant message?

Do I need to prepare for my first meeting?

How should I respond to this email?

Should I try to find Joan in person, call her, or write back to her email?

Do I have anything to bring up at our team meeting?

Should I say this thought right now?

Do I agree or disagree with that point?

Should I say this thought right now?

Do I agree or disagree with that point?

Do I have time for a quick break before my next meeting?

Should I check email now?

Should I respond to this email?

How should I respond to this email?

How should I respond to *this* email?

Should I check voicemail now?

Do I feel like a snack?

What do I feel like eating?

Should I get a bowl of yogurt, order a breakfast sandwich, or get a chocolate milk?

Do I want to add granola, berries, or flaxseed to this yogurt?

Are the credit card points worth paying with credit for this?

Do I need napkins?

Should I go talk to Todd sitting by the window?

Which route should I take back up if I want to chat with Joan?

What should I say to her about the meeting?

Do I agree or disagree with Jamie's plan?

What should I propose as a next step?

Should I stop at the bathroom or head to my desk?

Should I check email now?

Should I attend the total company meeting?

Should I see if anybody wants to sit together?

Should I sit at the front or the back?

Should I check my email?

Should I respond to this email now?

Do I need to do anything to prepare for my next meeting?

What's my proposal going to be in this next meeting?

Should I check email now?

How should I spend the two hours I have open after this next meeting?

Should I walk around the building and visit my client groups?

Should I check email now?

Which way should I go?

Should I check email now?

What's the best answer to that question?

Should I check email now?

Should I tell Mark about the feedback from his team?

How should I tell him?

Should I check email now?

Should I check email now?

Should I check email now?

Should I check email now?

Should I check email now?

Should I check email now?

How should I spend the next hour and a half?

Should I check email now?

Should I do this or that?

Should I check email now?

Should I check email now?

Should I respond to this email?

Should I check email now?

Should I check email now?

Should I check email now?

Should I get lunch from the cafeteria or go out for lunch?

Should I see if anyone wants to get lunch together or just go myself?

Should I check email now?

Do I want a turkey sandwich, roast beef sandwich, ham sandwich, egg salad sandwich, tuna salad sandwich, or cheese sandwich?

Do I want it on brown bread, white bread, multigrain bread, rye bread, olive bread, or in a pita?

Do I want it toasted?

Do I want mayo?

Do I want mustard?

Do I want tomatoes?

Do I want onions?

Do I want pickles?

Do I want lettuce?

Do I want cheese?

Do I want extra meat or is this enough?

Do I want salt and pepper?

Do I want it to go or for here?

Do I want anything else with this?

Do I want soup?

Do I want beef barley or split pea?

Do I want to get in the left line or the right line?

Should I check email now?

Do I want to pay with cash, credit, or debit?

Do I need any utensils?

Should I take plastic utensils or metal utensils?

How many napkins should I take?

Where should I eat?

Should I check email now?

Should I email Leslie now?

What should we have for dinner tonight?

Do we have chicken or fish in the freezer, or would takeout be easier?

Do I need anything to prepare for my next meeting?

Should I ask what the agenda is for this meeting?

Should I say something, since I disagree with that point?

Should I say something, since I disagree with *that* point?

Should I try to summarize the meeting and get everyone aligned on next steps?

Should I go back to my desk or talk to Ashley about the meeting?

Should I check email now?

Should I check voicemail now?

How should I spend the next three hours?

What time should I try to leave work today to meet Leslie for dinner?

Should I check email now?

How should I respond to this email?

Should I ask my boss for guidance on this email?

Should I go talk to Sean face-to-face instead?

What should we do tonight?

Should we try to visit my parents this weekend?

Should we try to visit Leslie's parents this weekend?

Should we try to visit my sister this weekend?

What should I have for a snack?

Should I have almonds from my desk or buy something from the cafeteria?

Should I have cheese, carrot sticks, or a chocolate milk?

Should I pay with cash or credit card?

Do I need to take napkins up to my desk?

Which way should I walk back so I can talk to Mark?

Should I check email now?

Should I work on the change project or spend the rest of the day answering emails?

Should I work on the change project at my desk or book a room?

When should we make the promotion announcement?

How should we word the announcement?

Should I mention her education?

Do I need to send the announcement to anyone for approval?

Do I need to get anything done before going home?

Do I need to do any work tonight for any meetings tomorrow?

Do I need to take my laptop home tonight for anything else?

Do I need to talk to Amanda before I leave?

Is there any paperwork I need to finish with Tanya before I leave?

Which route should I take home?

Should I listen to the radio to check the traffic report?

Should I call my parents from the car?

Should I see if they're free this weekend or next?

Should I stay on the highway or take the side streets?

Should I turn left at Bathurst or continue to Spadina?

Do I have time to stop at the post office to check my PO Box?

What do I need to get done tonight before bed?

What time should we try to go to sleep?

What kind of salad can I make?

Should I set the table with candles and place mats or should we eat casually on the counter?

What should we talk about over dinner?

How can I support her through that situation?

What ideas for the weekend should I propose?

Who should do the dishes and who should clean up the kitchen?

Should I check email now?

Should I see if Leslie wants to go for a walk or go to yoga after dinner?

Do I have time to write?

Should I write at home or at a coffee shop?

Should I check email now?

Should I stay up a bit later to read?

What time should I set my alarm for in the morning?

Do I plan to go to the gym?

What meetings do I have tomorrow that I need to think about?

285 reasons why you're tired right now

What a day!

In total I made **285** decisions. Exhausting. What were they about? I'm embarrassed to admit I made **75** decisions at the gym, **62** decisions about checking email, and **32** decisions about food.

These three topics alone were half of all my daily decisions, yet they were things that didn't really matter. Sure, it's great to go to the gym. But there's no reason I couldn't studiously follow a written workout. Sure, part of my job is being responsive. But I would still be responsive if I checked email twice a day in fifteen-minute windows instead of as "brain padding" whenever I found a spare minute. And I love food. I never want to skip meals. I never want to eat at my desk. But a preset shake every morning with dinner leftovers every lunch would give me food I love and save thirty-two decisions.

What does all this decision-making do?

Why was I so tired when I got home at night?

Turns out the answers were right in front of me.

What do you find every morning and lose every night?

Imagine you start every morning with a bright yellow sponge firmly implanted in your brain. Sounds painful, but good news, it's a magic sponge! This bright yellow sponge makes all your decisions for you. Just like that! Make a decision? A little chunk of sponge cracks off. This happens throughout the day. And what happens when the sponge is completely gone? You're spongeless. You can't make decisions. And there are only two ways to regrow your sponge: food and sleep.

Until you eat or sleep, you are mindless and ripe for making bad decisions.

John Tierney is the *New York Times*–bestselling coauthor of *Willpower: Rediscovering the Greatest Human Strength.* He says: "Decision fatigue helps explain why ordinarily sensible people get angry at colleagues and families, splurge on clothes, buy junk food at the supermarket and can't resist the dealer's offer to rustproof their new car. No matter how rational and high-minded you try to be, you can't make decision after decision without paying a biological price. It's different from ordinary physical fatigue—you're not consciously aware of being tired—but you're low on mental energy."

Many people are familiar with the painful process of walking around a giant department store and picking items for a wedding registry. When Leslie and I went to Hudson's Bay at 10:00 a.m. on a Saturday morning, we were full of energy. Yellow bowls or blue bowls? Dark yellow or light yellow? Shiny or not that shiny? What about glasses? Should we get eight or twelve? Heavy or light? Do we need tall and short or just tall or just short? What design? What about wineglasses? Do we need twelve as well? What shape? What brand of blender? How many blankets? How many pillows? How many towels? What color towels? By the end we were exhausted. Our sponges had disintegrated. I remember the clerk asking if we wanted to add a $300 ice bucket at the end of our trip and us nodding with glassy eyes and our mouths hanging open.

"Once you're mentally depleted, you become reluctant to make trade-offs," John says, "which involve a particularly advanced and taxing form of decision making . . . To compromise is a complex human ability and therefore one of the first to decline when willpower is depleted . . . If you're shopping, you're liable to look at only one dimension, like price: just give me the cheapest . . . Decision fatigue leaves you vulnerable to marketers who know how to time their sales . . . And this isn't the only reason that sweet snacks are featured prominently at the cash register, just when shoppers are depleted after all their decisions in the aisles. With their willpower reduced, they're more likely to yield to any kind of temptation, but they're especially vulnerable to candy and soda and anything else offering a quick hit of sugar."

The only person whose rules you have no choice but to follow

I struggled investing money for years.

I read a book on how to do it myself and knew I had to try carving off a small percentage of income, move it to an investing account, and put it in a diversified fund. There was no reason not to invest! But at the end of the year, every year, any money I tried setting aside was just sitting there. Not invested. No increases, no dividends, no nothing. Just getting eaten away by inflation.

I felt stupid, lazy, and forgetful.

What was wrong with me?

I looked back and found a horrible case of decision fatigue had set in without me realizing it. When this happens people have only two options:

1. Make no decision.
2. Make a bad decision.

My bank didn't have an automatic investing feature, so I had to do it myself. I set a calendar reminder on the first of every month to try to move some money into investments, but . . . whenever the first of the month hit, something happened. I looked at the price of the fund and if it had risen over the previous day, week, or month, I said to myself, "Oh, I don't want to buy it now. It's too expensive. I'll wait a couple of days until it comes down." Then I'd keep checking the price every day, multiple times a day. Occasionally it would come down and I'd buy some. But sometimes it would keep rising. So I'd watch it go up and keep telling myself I'd buy it as soon as it came back down. If it was $50 one day, $51 the next, and $52 the next, then even if it dropped down to $51, I'd tell myself it wasn't as cheap as when I started, so I had to keep waiting. Eventually a month would pass and my calendar reminder would go off telling me it was time to invest again. But I hadn't invested for last month yet! So I now had two months saved up, which meant my decision on when to invest was even more important.

My brain was feeling a tremendous amount of options around making these investment decisions. And I was just trying to buy one fund. I couldn't overcome this fear. Soon another month had piled up. Then another. Anxiety set in about my failure to invest anything, and I called my friend Fred one night in a panic.

Fred studied economics under John Nash at Princeton, worked in investment banking for years, and, more important, was someone I trusted enough to share my financial failures with.

"I had the same problem," he said. "Then I made rules for myself. I have three rules. I wrote them down on a piece of paper, which I leave at my desk. I follow the three rules even if I don't want to."

Rule #1: If Checking Account > $1,000, Move All $ over $1,000 into Investing Account.

Rule #2: If Investing Account > $1,000, Move All $ over $1,000 into Investments.

Rule #3: Never Break Rule #1 or Rule #2.

"It works because I remove my brain from the equation. I don't have any choice, so I'm forced to be happy with how I've invested. If the fund went up in value, I tell myself I was smart for investing some earlier to capitalize on those gains! Like, if the market is at an all-time high and there has never been a worse time to buy, I tell myself, 'Boy, I sure am smart only investing a little now and not my entire life savings.' Alternatively, if the fund has gone down in value, I tell myself I was smart for saving money to benefit from lower prices today. It's a win-win. Now all my money is invested, I don't pay any adviser fees, and I don't spend any time thinking about it."

Rules. Limits. Barriers. Creating mental brick walls to stop making decisions. Like the fish department with all the choices removed. Why can't we make rules for our own brain? Preserve our decision-making energy for decisions that matter. A guided workout at the gym. A preset breakfast shake.

What happens when we give ourselves less choice?

The unanticipated joy of being totally stuck

Daniel Gilbert, author of *Stumbling on Happiness*, wondered this, too. He gave a TED Talk about an experiment he ran on the Harvard campus:

> We created a photography course, a black-and-white photography course, and we allowed students to come in and learn how to use a darkroom. So we gave them cameras, they went around campus, they took twelve pictures of their favorite professors and their dorm room and their dog. They bring us the camera, we make up a contact sheet, they figure out which are the two best pictures, and

we now spend six hours teaching them about darkrooms. And they blow two of them up and they have two gorgeous eight-by-ten glossies of meaningful things to them and we say, "Which one would you like to give up?" They say, "I have to give one up?" And we say, "Oh, yes, we need one as evidence of the class project. So you have to give me one. You have to make a choice. You get to keep one, and I get to keep one."

Now, there are two conditions in this experiment. In one case, the students are told, "But you know, if you want to change your mind, I'll always have the other one here, and in the next four days, before I actually mail it to headquarters, I'll be glad to swap it out with you . . . Better yet, I'll check with you. You ever want to change your mind, it's totally returnable." The other half of the students are told the exact opposite. "Make your choice. And by the way, the mail is going out, gosh, in two minutes, to England. Your picture will be winging its way over the Atlantic. You will never see it again." Now, half of the students . . . are asked to make predictions about how much they're going to come to like the picture they keep and the picture they leave behind. Other students are just sent back to their little dorm rooms and they are measured . . . on their liking and satisfaction with the picture. And look at what we find.

First of all . . . [the students] think they're going to maybe come to like the picture they chose a little more than the one they left behind, but these are not statistically significant differences. It's a very small increase, and it doesn't much matter whether they were in the reversible or irreversible condition.

Wrong-o. Bad simulators. Because here's what's really happening. Both right before the swap and five days later, people who are stuck with that picture, who have no choice, who can never change their mind, like it a lot. And people who are deliberating—"Should I return it? Have I gotten the right one? Maybe this isn't the good one? Maybe I left the good one?"—have killed themselves. They don't like their picture, and in fact even after the opportunity to swap has expired, they still don't like their picture. Why? Because the (reversible) condition is not conducive to the synthesis of happiness.

So here's the final piece of this experiment. We bring in a whole new group of naive Harvard students and we say, "You know, we're doing a photography course, and we can do it one of two ways. We could do it so that when you take the two pictures, you'd have four days to change your mind, or we're doing another course where you take the two pictures and you make up your mind right away and you can never change it. Which course would you like to be in?" Duh! Sixty-six percent of the students—two-thirds—prefer to be in the course where they have the opportunity to change their mind. Hello? Sixty-six percent of the students choose to be in the course in which they will ultimately be deeply dissatisfied with the picture.

No wonder we are exhausted from making decisions. Because we *want* to make those decisions. We want to go to the movie theater with the most movies playing, we like the restaurant with the long menu, we want the shoe store with the most shoes. But having more choice reduces our happiness. We get decision fatigue. What happens? We avoid the decision or we make a bad decision. And we always worry we made the wrong choice. This is why I always failed to invest any money. It's why, looking back at our wedding registry, Leslie and I wondered who picked some of the things on there. We had to go through it all again with fresh sponges.

"Freedom and autonomy are critical to our well-being, and choice is critical to freedom and autonomy," says Barry Schwartz, author of *The Paradox of Choice*. "Nonetheless, though modern Americans have more choice than any group of people ever has before, and thus, presumably, more freedom and autonomy, we don't seem to be benefiting from it psychologically."

4 simple words that will help you prioritize everything

You make fewer decisions. You do some ten times faster, some five times faster, and some many times longer. But it all adds up to quicker decisions and focusing on what's important. You look at decisions you make on a daily basis and decide which ones to **automate**, **regulate**, **effectuate**, and **debate**.

Ruby WatchCo. is one of the most popular restaurants in Toronto—ranked in the top ten of thousands in the city—and run by celebrity chef Lynn Crawford. Before opening the restaurant, Lynn worked as executive chef at the Manhattan Four Seasons, starred in *Restaurant Makeover*, and wrote two bestselling cookbooks.

Her restaurant operates like no other in the city!

Reservations are taken at only two seating times, it's a flat fifty bucks per person, and the four-course prix fixe menu changes every day. What else is available besides the four-course prix fixe menu? Nothing! There are no other choices. Nothing else to eat, no menus to choose from, no prices to think about. And everybody gets dessert. For the kitchen, there are only allergies to accommodate—cooking is streamlined, dishes all the same size, waste is limited, and checks added quickly for faster turnaround.

Everything arrives "family-style" in big dishes at the center of the table, and the dimly lit chattery dining room is packed every night of the week. *The Globe and Mail* says, "It's nice for the chef, who gets to be spontaneous. Also very nice for the chef to give up that whole challenge of offering different menu items, as the cost and stress of both stocking and cooking different foods is eliminated. It's so much easier!"

Lynn says, "The decision of what to choose at a restaurant can be overwhelming. I'm thrilled when someone says, 'Let me cook for you.'"

Delaying is gone. Choosing nothing is gone! And businesses like Lynn's restaurant can benefit.

Guess what Stanford researcher Sheena Iyengar reports Procter & Gamble found when they chopped the varieties of Head & Shoulders on the shelf from twenty-six to fifteen? When you remove half the number of bottles the customers sees, your sales must go down, right? Nope, they got a sales increase of 10%.

When we are presented with too many decisions, we either:

Do nothing. Our brains are exhausted, so we stop making decisions completely. We walk out in protest! This is what happens on forms where you need to pick one of twenty-five different investment funds for your pension or twenty-six varieties of shampoo. What do people do? Ignore them all. Go with the default. We are so tired by this point we quit completely.

Do poorly. Don't feel like quitting? Well, there is another option. Making a decision that stinks. Being so exhausted you pick something, anything, just to get the decision-making done. Adding a $300 ice bucket to your wedding registry. Grabbing a king-size Oh Henry! at the end of your grocery shop. Easiest over best.

Your brain is the world's most valuable piece of real estate. It produces world-changing ideas, creates beautiful art, and explores great mysteries of life. But trivial decisions and endless choices buzz in front of your brain all day. They're flashing lights. Preventing you from pushing deeper. How can—ding!—think about—ping!—when all you're—ring! Endless decisions steal your deep thoughts.

Tiny decisions squat on your primo lot rent-free. They don't pay. They don't apologize. They just steal your brainpower. Sure, a lot of this comes from our increasingly connected world. Nicholas Carr, author of *New York Times* bestseller *The Shallows*, says, "The Net's interactivity gives us powerful new tools for finding information, expressing ourselves, and conversing with others. It also turns us into lab rats constantly pressing levers to get tiny pellets of social or intellectual nourishment."

I made 285 decisions on an average day. My brain was contemplating, weighing, evaluating, and deciding every minute I was awake.

But there is a secret. A secret to removing choice and making every decision at twice the speed.

After studying personal leadership traits among successful Ivy League grads, Fortune 500 CEOs, and bestselling authors, I slowly discovered the most successful people use the same secret to rid their brains of all the extra weight of hundreds of decisions a day.

It's simple.

The Just Do It Scribble.

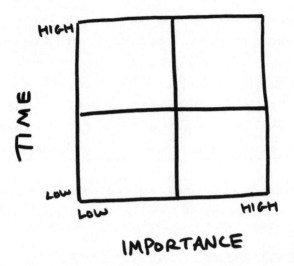

There it is. That simple. Every decision you make sits somewhere in this box.

It takes a little time . . . or a lot! It's not very important . . . or it's a big deal!

Here, let me fill it in for you.

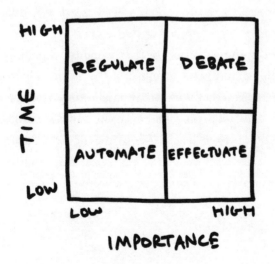

Automate—Buying toilet paper and detergent. Paying the phone bill. Deciding your route to work. Picking your workout routine. If it's low in time and low in importance, your goal is to automate. Outsource your brain completely and don't think about it again. Set online refills to ship toilet paper and detergent monthly. Set up auto bill payments from your bank account. Download a traffic-maps app and mindlessly follow the best route to work. And set a workout schedule and follow it. Free your brain. Just don't mistake these smaller decisions for the more important decisions in which they reside. Deciding to work out every day is important. Picking which dumbbell to lift next is not.

Effectuate—Grabbing the kids from day care. Eating dinner with the family every night. Saying hi to your team every morning. Effectuate is a big word with a simple meaning: Git 'er done. Nail it. Just do it. If it's low in time but high in importance, your goal is to just do it. There is no decision to make. Simply effectuate.

Regulate—Checking email. Managing your calendar. Doing chores. If it's high in time and low in importance, your goal is to regulate. Make rules and follow them. Set an email window. A single calendar review meeting. A chores blitz every Sunday morning instead of painfully doing one or two a day.

Debate—Buying a house. Picking a spouse. Applying for a job. Moving. High-importance, high-time decisions are the ones to spend the most time on. Debate in your head, call trusted friends, list the pros and cons. Slow the decision down to molasses so you can engage in a proper debate. These are the ones that matter.

Automate, Regulate, and Effectuate all remove decisions from your head.

What are you left with?

Debate.

Deep thinking, questioning, wondering.

Weighing big decisions that matter in order to avoid making bad ones.

Every now and then, thinking about the decisions in your life and writing them down in this box will help sort out for yourself what matters and what doesn't. What can you Automate so you never think about it again? What can you Regulate so you do it in set times and windows? What can you Effectuate as something you simply just do? And what can you Debate—what big thoughts can you chew on to make sure you're doing the right thing?

Over time you will do this *automatically*, without thinking about it. You will have developed the muscle to automatically chunk out your decisions.

Now, the secret isn't perfect. Sometimes small decisions will leak out and become big deals in your head. But that's okay. The goal is not to be perfect. The goal is just to be better than before. Automating, regulating, and effectuating free your mind and free your time.

Your aching brain will thank you.

5

Removal #2: The counterintuitive way to have more time

When I was fourteen years old, I got my first job in a nepotism-riddled scandal. My cousin Anita let me work as a pharmacy technician in her tiny six-hundred-square-foot pharmacy in small-town Ontario. It was the size of a large closet and located at the front door of a busy medical building with a walk-in clinic with lineups of coughing children streaming out the door all day. Even though it was tiny, the pharmacy filled hundreds of prescriptions a day, in a nonstop, adrenaline-rushing assembly-line atmosphere. Prescriptions were dropped off, pills counted, and advice dispensed, sometimes in less than a minute. Screaming babies, snotty toddlers, and drugged-out moms were crammed together in a sardine tin of throat infections.

I started in a white lab coat with a three-hour Friday-night shift. Backbreaking. Anita figured I couldn't do much damage on the slowest time of the week, so I was given a chance to perfect my pill counting with slightly shorter lines. Every Friday I worked those three hours, got a ride in my dad's station wagon to Subway for a salami sub on white bread, then went home to watch Scully and Mulder do their thing on *The X-Files*.

Now, when you have only six hundred square feet of space, you only have six hundred square feet of space. Elbows touched and hips bumped all day, and cold sandwiches were eaten on dirty footstools in the corner. Pill bottles were stashed above and below the counter, a tiny fridge and microwave wedged above the tiny sink, and you had to walk through the accountant's paperwork piles to get to the bathroom—which was stuffed with coats and boots. And try not to pee on the pyramids of ginger ale cases stacked on both sides of the toilet.

The place did well, so my cousin teamed up with my dad to open a second location twenty minutes away. "This time," they said, "we'll actually have room to move." So they built the second store three times the size of the first. There was enough shelf space to actually have greeting cards and sunblock and bandages, and the staff could move freely, like ballet dancers at the Met. Lots of air, shelves everywhere.

I turned sixteen and started working at the second store as my summer job. I had perfected counting pills now and had worked up the courage to talk to customers. I had also grown a wispy mustache, so I no longer looked like an eleven-year-old in Coke-bottle glasses behind the counter. Now I looked thirteen.

I noticed immediately that the second store was worse than the first in almost every way.

First off, there was no extra storage space. Where was the extra storage space? Every shelf was full and boxes were stuffed above and below the counter. Because there were more items on the shelves, there was more overstock of more items, so now you had to watch so you didn't pee onto canes or greeting cards beside the toilet.

Communication was more difficult, too. Messages were passed on paper and notebooks instead of the tiny staff just talking amongst themselves. There was room for two computers now, which led to nice-looking drop-off and pickup stations instead of just one spot. But that meant customer confusion and time lost moving everything between two spots. The extra distance also meant customers sometimes felt nobody was around when they wanted to drop off a prescription. And when their pills were ready you now had to call them or find them down an aisle. So the pharmacist took more time giving out prescriptions. Prescriptions took longer to fill. Everybody was working as fast as they could, but it felt slow to customers.

What happened?

Work expands to fill the space available and the result is lower quality.

Although this story seems like it's about having more space, it's actually about having more time. With longer counters, twice the drop-offs, and more room for customers to walk around, the new store offered more time to fill prescriptions. So it took more time. Have you ever got a prescription filled in the middle of a gigantic warehouse store? Takes a while, doesn't it?

The single law that determines how long anything takes to do

In November 1955 a strange article appeared in *The Economist* by an unknown writer named C. Northcote Parkinson. Readers who started skimming the article, titled "Parkinson's Law," were met with sarcastic, biting paragraphs poking sharp holes in government bureaucracy and mocking ever-expanding corporate structures. It was searing criticism masked as an information piece. It began innocently enough with the following paragraph:

> It is a commonplace observation that work expands so as to fill the time available for its completion. Thus, an elderly lady of leisure can spend the entire day in writing and dispatching a postcard to her niece at Bognor Regis. An hour will be spent in finding the postcard, another in hunting for spectacles, half-an-hour in a search for the ad-

dress, an hour and a quarter in composition, and twenty minutes in deciding whether or not to take an umbrella when going to the pillar-box in the next street. The total effort which would occupy a busy man for three minutes all told may in this fashion leave another person prostrate after a day of doubt, anxiety and toil.

The thesis of the piece was in the first sentence: "It is a commonplace observation that work expands so as to fill the time available for its completion."

Haven't we heard advice like this before? "The ultimate inspiration is the deadline," for instance. "If you leave it till the last minute, it takes only a minute to do." Or how about: "The contents of your purse will expand to fill all available space."

In the second pharmacy that my cousin opened, there was more time available. Customers weren't staring at you. There was no walk-in clinic next door outputting prescription after prescription, so there was time to look up research and answer questions about cough syrup. It was a calm environment as opposed to a hectic environment. And work expanded to fill this time.

Think back to bringing homework home from school on the weekends. There was nothing better than a weekend! But the dull pain of having to do a page of math problems and write a book summary loomed like a faint black cloud over Friday night, all day Saturday, and Sunday morning. I remember I would always work on homework Sunday night. But once in a while, if we were going away for the weekend, if I had busy plans on both days, I would actually get my homework done on Friday night. The deadline had artificially become sooner in my mind. And what happened? It felt great. It felt like I had more time all weekend. A fake early deadline created more space.

How do you cut all meeting time in half?

As part of a job I had a few years ago I suddenly took ownership over the company's weekly meeting for all employees. It was a rambly Friday-morning affair without a clear agenda, presentation guidelines, or timelines, all in front of a thousand people. The CEO would speak for as long as he wanted about whatever he wanted and then pass the mic to the next executive sitting at a table, who would speak as long as he wanted about whatever he wanted, before passing the mic to the next person. It was unpredictable—and starting at 9:00 a.m., it rolled into 10:00 a.m., sometimes 10:30 a.m., and occasionally 11:00 a.m. People would go on tangents. Nobody was concise. And everyone would leave two hours later in a daze, trying to remember all the mixed priorities they heard at the beginning of the meeting.

So I worked with the CEO to redesign the meeting. We created five segments of five minutes each and set up an agenda and schedule of presenters in advance. "The Numbers," "Outside Our Walls," "The Basics 101," "Sell! Sell! Sell!" and "Mailbag," where the CEO opened letters and answered questions from the audience.

The new meeting was twenty-five minutes long!

And it never went over time once.

How come?

Because I downloaded a "dong" sound effect that we played over the speakers with one minute left, a "ticking clock" sound effect that played with fifteen seconds left, and then the A/V guys actually *cut off a person's microphone* when time hit zero. If you hit zero, you would be talking onstage but nobody could hear you. You just had to walk off.

What happened?

Well, at first everybody complained. "I need seven minutes to present," "I need ten minutes," "I need much, much longer because I have something very, very important to say." We said no and shared this quote from a *Harvard Business Review* interview with former GE CEO Jack Welch:

"For a large organization to be effective, it must be simple. For a large organization to be simple, its people must have self-confidence and intellectual self-assurance. Insecure managers create complexity. Frightened, nervous managers use thick, convoluted planning books and busy slides filled with everything they've known since childhood. Real leaders don't need clutter. People must have the self-confidence to be clear, precise, to be sure that every person in their organization—highest to lowest—understands what the business is trying to achieve. But it's not easy. You can't believe how hard it is for people to be simple, how much they fear being simple. They worry that if they're simple, people will think they're simple-minded. In reality, of course, it's just the reverse. Clear, tough-minded people are the most simple."

Then what happened?

Well, with a clear time limit, presenters practiced! They timed themselves. They prioritized their most important messages and scrapped everything else. They used bullet points and summary slides. We introduced the concept by saying "If you can't say it concisely in five minutes, you can't say it. By then people doze off or start checking their email." Have you ever tried listening to someone talk for twenty straight minutes? Unless they are extremely clear, concise, and captivating, it's a nightmare.

Everybody got a bit scared of their mic cutting off, so the meetings were always twenty-five minutes.

What happened to productivity?

Well, a thousand people saved an hour every week. That's 2.5% of *total company time* saved with just one small change.

How do you complete a three-month project in one day?

Sam Raina is a leader in the technology industry. He oversees the design and development of a large website with millions of hits a day. He has more than sixty people working for him. It's a big team. There are many moving parts. From designers to coders to copy editors. How does he motivate his team to design and launch entirely new pages for the website from scratch?

He follows Parkinson's Law and cuts down time.

He books his entire team for secret one-day meetings and then issues them a challenge in the morning that he says they're going to get done by the end of the day. There is only one day to make an entire website! From designing to layout to testing—everything. Everyone freaks out about the deadline. And then everyone starts working together.

"The less time we have to do it, the more focused and organized we are. We all work together. We have to! There is no way we'd hit the deadline otherwise. And we always manage to pull it off," Sam says.

By spending a day on a project that would otherwise take months, he frees up everyone's thinking time, transactional time, and work time. Nobody will be thinking about the website in the bed, bath, or bus again. They can think about other things! There will be no emails about the website, no out-of-office messages, no meetings set up to discuss it, no confusion about who said what. Everyone talks in person. At the same time. Until it's done!

What's the counterintuitive secret to having more time?

Chop the amount of time you have to do it.

Look at the left of the graph. The less time available, the more effort you put in. There is no choice. The deadline is right here. Think of how focused you are in an exam. Two hours to do it? You do it in two hours! That deadline creates an urgency that allows the mind to prioritize and focus.

Now look at the right of the graph. The more time available, the less effort we put in overall. A little thought today. Start the project tomorrow. Revisit it next week. We procrastinate. Why? Because we're allowed to. There is no penalty. Nothing kills productivity faster than a late deadline.

What does C. Northcote Parkinson say about waiting to get it done? "Delay is the deadliest form of denial," he says.

Have you ever finished a project on time and then the teacher announces to the class that the deadline has been extended? What a bummer. Now, even though you finished at the original deadline, you get the pain and torture of mentally revisiting your project over and over again until you hand it in. Could it be better? How can we improve it?

Calvin says it best:

Remember: Work expands to fill the time available for its completion. At my cousin's second pharmacy, in the original thousand-person company meeting, in a normal website-development cycle, what invisible liability do you find? **Time.** Too much of it. And work expanding to fill it as a result.

What's the solution?

Create last-minute panic!

Move deadlines up, revise them for yourself, and remember you are creating space after the project has been delivered. Remember: A late deadline is painful. Nothing gets done.

Do only nerds do their homework Friday night?

Maybe.

But they're the ones with the whole weekend to party.

6

Removal #3: How to add an hour to a day with only one small change

got my first office job in my early twenties.

For four months between school years in college I held the sexy job title of "summer intern" at a big consulting company in a downtown high-rise. Casey was my boss and the head of the project I was assigned to for the summer, which was for one of the world's largest oil and gas companies.

One Monday morning, I was sitting in his glass-windowed corner office with the rising sun beaming onto the desk between us. More than three months of late-night stress and working on weekends had finally rolled up to right now.

We were minutes away from our big presentation.

Casey's sense of humor had carried me through all the challenges and Chinese takeout boxes leading up to today, but he had just asked me a last-minute question that made me snap. My nerves were frayed. I had no energy left.

"Why do we have an assumption in here instead of an actual figure?" he asked.

"Because Roger didn't write back to my three emails asking him for the right number and he never gave us a number where we could call him. I tried his assistant twice and never heard back, either. It's like he forgot we existed. You know that."

Roger was the highly touted CEO of the oil and gas company who everybody looked up to. He was highlighted in flashy magazine articles and known as a people leader who espoused work-life balance while nonchalantly beating his numbers every year. Meanwhile, employees at the company told us he ate lunch in the company cafeteria, drove a beat-up truck to work, and had dinner with his kids every night.

The man was a legend.

After our introductory meeting three months back I wrote Roger an email summarizing our meeting and next steps. He didn't write back. I then took my laptop home every night in case Roger emailed with an urgent question or request. I checked email every half an hour just in case the CEO of the company ever emailed late at night asking for a project update the next morning. Just so if he ever needed something, anything, I'd be there.

But . . . there was nothing. In three months of working for him he didn't write me a single email. He didn't write Casey any emails, either. We dropped a few questions along the way but never heard back. And I had just told Casey my messages to his assistant weren't returned, either. Now suddenly it was time for our big presentation and Casey was questioning why I didn't have certain numbers.

I steadied my nerves as we stepped into the boardroom where Roger was sitting and chatting with our company president. He smiled and got up to shake our hands and thank us for the work we'd done. "I'm so excited," he said with a big grin. "I can't tell you how much I appreciate how hard you've been working. You guys are geniuses. I'm going to learn so much from this chat."

The anger I felt about his unresponsiveness suddenly melted. I felt like a million bucks.

We jumped into the presentation and had a great discussion. It was casual, engaging, and open. He loved it. And I couldn't believe how relaxed everything felt. He was talking to us like old friends. After the meeting was done there was so much trust between us. So as we were packing up, I thought about it for a split second and decided to ask him one last question.

I couldn't help myself.

"Roger, thanks so much for today. We had trouble running some numbers by you in advance. And I know we didn't hear from you on the additional questions we had. So, just for my own learning, can I ask why you don't write or respond to emails? How do you do that?"

His eyes opened a bit and he seemed surprised by the question. But he wasn't fazed.

"Neil," he said, "there's a problem with email. After you send one, the responsibility of it goes away from you and becomes the responsibility of the other person. It's a hot potato. An email is work given to you by somebody else."

I nodded, thinking about all the emails I got from Casey and coworkers.

"I do read emails, but the ones looking for something are always much less urgent than they seem. When I don't respond, one of two things happens:

1. The person figures it out on their own, or,
2. They email me again because it really was important.

"Sure, I send one or two emails a day, but they usually say, 'Give me a call,' or, 'Let's chat about this.' Unless they're from my wife. I answer all of those."

I was very confused.

How was the CEO of a multibillion-dollar company with thousands of employees not emailing?

He paused to look at me and sensed I didn't get it.

"You know what," he continued, "since I don't write many emails, I don't receive many, either. I probably only get five or ten emails a day."

Five emails a day? Here I was working at a consulting company writing emails morning, noon, and night. It was the same for everyone. "My inbox has seven hundred emails," my coworkers would say and sigh. "I did emails all Sunday afternoon." There was no way around it. After all, our bosses sent urgent emails at 7:00 a.m. Saturday, late Sunday afternoon, or 11:00 p.m. Friday. I knew this was common in my company and others. McKinsey had even reported that office workers spend on average 28% of their time answering email. Almost a third. And Baydin, one of the world's largest email-management services, says the average person gets 147 emails a day. We were all attached to our cell phones and computers, firing emails around, working hard to get everything done. It was part of the job. And we all wanted to do a good job.

Suddenly it started to click why Roger was known to have lunch in the cafeteria with employees every day and drive home for dinner with his family every night.

He didn't respond to hot potatoes.

He didn't write back to emails and create email chains.

I looked up at Roger again, and he continued.

"Most of the time, Neil, people really do figure it out on their own. They realize they know the answer, they keep on moving, they develop confidence for next time. They become better themselves. Your assumptions in the slides today weren't perfect, but they worked perfectly well and you learned by doing them. Don't get me wrong. I sometimes walk over to chat with a person or pick up the phone. But if I wrote back to an email, I'd be sending a hot potato. And nobody wants to be asked by the CEO to do something . . .

never mind on an evening or weekend. Why? Because people would drop everything to reply. And they would expect me to reply to that. Basically, if I sent an email, it would never end. So I end it."

How to protect your most valuable asset

You have only one brain. And it focuses on only one thing at one time.

Your brain is the most incredible and complex object in the universe. We have never seen anything like it. We barely understand it. We use it, but we don't know how we use it. When we kick, we pull our leg back and swing it forward. When we think, we just think. As Cliff once said on *Cheers*, "Interesting little article here. It says the average human being only uses seventeen percent of his brain. Boy, you realize what that means? We don't use a full, uh . . . sixty-four percent."

Your brain is capable of infinite possibilities: producing great works of art, building businesses, raising children. Brains made *The Starry Night* and the Great Wall of China. The Beatles and the Bible. Brains made planes, trains, and automobiles. Brains make your life what it is and die when you do. The good news is for no money down, no annual fees, and no monthly interest, you get one free copy of the universe's most complex and powerful object. It's yours for life! The only bad news is there is no warranty, it requires daily recharging, and even the longest-lasting models in the world last only forty thousand days. (The average model lasts twenty-five thousand days.)

You break it, it's broken. Seat belts, bike helmets, and exercise are mandatory. For power, your brain recharges with six to eight hours of sleep a day and as much healthy food as possible. That's a lot of gas! It takes the equivalent of more than sixteen apples a day just to power your brain. But remember: The world's most powerful supercomputer has been compacted into a three-pound pile of flesh in your skull, so no wonder it needs so much energy. Yes, nearly a full third of all the food you eat goes straight to powering your brain.

Roger was the smartest guy at the company. No doubt about it. In the years since, he's gone up and up and up. All while eating lunch in the cafeteria every day and dinner with his family every night. I had worked with Roger only three months when I learned how to add an hour to the day with only one small change.

How?

Block access. Protect your brain. Guard it. **Remove all entry points to your brain except a single one you can control.** In addition to Roger's approach to email, I learned later that he didn't have a desk phone, personal email address, or any social media accounts. Fuel your brain and let it run wild by removing access points. Close the doors and lock the windows, but answer the bell.

What's the bell? It's your number one top priority. What was Roger's bell? Emails from the chairman of the board and his family. Not voicemail, not texts, not anything else. Have you ever shopped in a small-town convenience store where they have a little bell on the front counter? They are busy stocking shelves. They are busy unpacking boxes. They are busy placing orders. But when you ring that bell they are right there, right away. That's what it means to close the doors and lock the windows but answer the bell.

Let your brain produce great work, savor space, and power your biggest ideas, most passionate efforts, and greatest accomplishments.

The greatest misconception you share
with every other employee

Multitasking.

Doing two or more things at once.

How often do you hear people use that word? What does it mean? And where did it even come from?

We have to go all the way back to a paper written by IBM in 1965 to find the origin of the word *multitasking*. How was it defined? "The ability of a microprocessor to apparently process several tasks simultaneously."

Yes, that is the actual meaning. Right from the paper. Want to read it again? This time let me underline one word.

"The ability of a microprocessor to <u>apparently</u> process several tasks simultaneously."

Apparently? Apparently! What do they mean by *apparently*? You mean, even computers don't *actually* process several tasks at the same time? Well, no. They don't. Another quote, another underline from me:

"Computer multitasking in single core microprocessors actually involves <u>time-sharing</u> the processor; only one task can actually be active at a time, but tasks are rotated through many times a second."

Time-sharing. We've heard of time-sharing. Like splitting a lake house with five other couples throughout the year. Everyone has the illusion of owning a lake house! But really, you're all just going at different times.

And this is for single-core microprocessors. Those with one brain. You know who else has one brain? You and me. We can make a dual-core computer, but we haven't developed a dual-brain baby yet. *That* kid will actually be able to multitask.

Now, I know what you might be thinking. Just because a computer doesn't *actually* do more than one task at once, who says you can't? After all, haven't you ever brushed your teeth while taking off your socks, texted while driving, or answered emails on a conference call?

No.

You haven't actually done any of those things.

You have taken tiny breaks from driving to text and you have taken tiny breaks from texting to drive. You have taken tiny breaks from brushing your teeth to remove your socks. You have taken tiny breaks from removing your socks to brush your teeth. Together, you may have accomplished all of it. But you have created only the illusion of multitasking.

As my friend Mike once told me, "Screwing up two things at the same time isn't multitasking."

Let's look at one final quote about multitasking in a computer's brain. This one comes from a white paper written by the company National Instruments:

"In the case of a computer with a single CPU core, only one task runs at any point in time, meaning that the CPU is actively executing instructions for that task. Multitasking solves the problem by scheduling which task may run at any given time and when another waiting task gets a turn. This act of reassigning a CPU from one task to another one is called a context switch. When context switches occur frequently enough, the illusion of parallelism is achieved."

When context switches occur frequently enough, the *illusion* of parallelism is achieved.

The single greatest misconception of every employee is that they can multitask. That their brains can do two things at once. But they can't. This is the illusion of parallelism. When jumping between many things is perfectly scheduled, everyone will think you're actually doing two things at the same time. But you're not. You're simply scheduling them in. Have you ever seen anybody checking emails while pressing "mute" on a conference call? They aren't listening to the call. But they said hello at the beginning and will "context switch" if anybody says their name. Like "Linda, what do you think of the proposal?" Suddenly Linda stops emailing and gives her two cents.

The illusion of parallelism is achieved.

Here's what it looks like in a *Dilbert* cartoon.

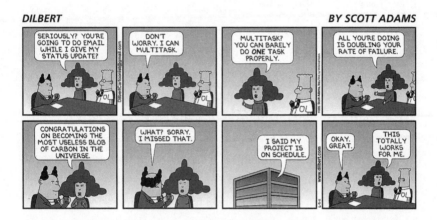

Do you remember when doctors were the only ones with pagers? Sometimes they were on call and they carried their pagers around. Sometimes they weren't on call and there was no way to reach them. If there was an emergency, the hospital would page the doctor and they'd drive over to deliver the baby or slice out the appendix. Emergency device for emergency situations. Then suddenly everyone had pagers. Then everyone had cell phones. Now everyone is accessible, any way, any time.

Do you remember when stores used to be closed on Sundays? It was family day. Church day. Quiet day. Nothing was open. You couldn't get anything done. Neither could anyone else. Then a few stores started opening on Sundays. Others wanted to compete. Local laws changed. Online stores opened twenty-four hours a day.

How do you add an hour to your day with only one small change? You need to remove access.

Close the doors, lock the windows, answer the bell.

The only two modes your brain actually has and how to use them

John Cleese, cofounder of Monty Python, knows a few things about removing access. Freeing your brain from the tyranny of "busy." He is famous for removing access and creating space in his life. What was the effect? Oh, not much. Just scoring Golden Globe and Academy Award nominations and being in *more than a hundred movies* all the way into his seventies.

As John described it in a speech to the organization Video Arts, we are in closed mode "most of the time when we're at work. We have inside us a feeling that there's lots to be done and we have to get on with it if we're going to get through it all. It's an active, probably slightly anxious mode, although the anxiety can be exciting and pleasurable . . . It's a mode in which we're very purposeful and it's a mode in which we can get very stressed and even a bit manic."

What's the opposite of this? John calls it open mode. That's where your brain is free and playful and capable of achieving greatness. Sound slightly counterintuitive? Maybe. But by closing off access to your brain . . . you're opening up your mind.

"By contrast," John says, "the open mode is a relaxed, expansive, less purposeful mode in which we're probably more contemplative, more inclined to humor . . . and consequently, more playful. It's a mode in which curiosity for its own sake can operate because we're not under pressure to get a specific thing done quickly. We can play and that is what allows our natural creativity to surface."

How do you get yourself into open mode? How do you block access?

"Let's take space," he says. "You can't become playful and therefore creative if you're under your usual pressures, because to cope with them you've got to be in the closed mode, right? So you have to create some space for yourself away from those demands. And that means sealing yourself off. You must make a quiet space for yourself where you will be undisturbed."

You must make a quiet space for yourself where you will be undisturbed.

One of the hardest and most important things you will ever do at work

How do you actually eliminate other outside disturbances? How do you cut off access . . . to yourself? Without building a shack in the middle of the forest.

It's not easy.

While working as Director of Leadership Development at Walmart, I counted six distinct ways people could communicate with me: email, voicemail, instant message, texting, written notes, and walking up to my desk. Every interruption took time because I suddenly had to do three things:

1. Bookmark
2. Prioritize
3. Switch

"People in a work setting," says psychologist David Meyer of the University of Michigan, "who are banging away on word processors at the same time they have to answer phones and talk to their co-workers or bosses—they're doing switches all the time. Not being able to concentrate for, say, tens of minutes at a time may mean it's costing a company as much as twenty to forty percent in terms of potential efficiency lost, or the 'time cost' of switching, as these researchers call it. In effect, you've got writer's block briefly as you go from one task to another. You've got to (a) want to switch tasks, you've got to (b) make the switch, and then you've got to (c) get warmed back up on what you're doing."

René Marois, a psychologist at Vanderbilt University, has done a study showing the brain exhibits a "response selection bottleneck." I like that! When someone calls me at the same time as an email comes in and a person walks up to my desk—what happens? Response selection bottleneck. Picture saying that in a robot voice. "Error. Response. Selection. Bottleneck." In other words, I get jammed up.

Another study from Harvard Business School is called "Rainmakers: Why Bad Weather Means Good Productivity" by Jooa Julia Lee, Francesca Gino, and Bradley R. Staats. They show that bad weather reduces our options of what we can do and *increases* our productivity. Less access to outside? More work done inside.

One day at work I decided to block off as much access to myself as possible. Close the doors. Lock the windows. But answer the bell. (For me the bell is emails from my boss.)

First, I logged in to my voicemail and permanently set it to "vacation mode" where it didn't allow callers to leave a voicemail. There was no beep. There would be no red light on my machine. I just left a message asking people to email me instead and then spelled out my email address really slowly a couple times.

Next, I deleted our office instant-messaging software and deleted my profile in the texting application we all used on our work phones. Coworkers used these to send messages because they came with the illusion of parallelism. But it was a red herring. Bookmark, prioritize, switch. No. I would never be in "away mode" anymore. I flat-out deleted it.

Last, I disabled all notifications from my email. No dings. No pop-ups. No reminders telling me an email arrived. With no voicemail, no text messages, no instant messages, and no email reminders, what happened? I created focus. And if I needed space from my own desk, I could go work in the cafeteria.

By cutting off access to myself, I was able to choose what to focus on, aim my brain at that task, and then nail it.

How do you add an hour to your day with only one small change?

Remove access. Close the doors. Lock the windows. And pick the bell you will answer and focus on. Delete and remove all access to yourself except for that one. Watch as your productivity spikes, your days become more productive, and you create beautiful space.

7

"What is this life if, full of care, we have no time to stand and stare?"

Why are we so busy?

Because we've run out of space.

And we don't always value space enough in our lives.

What's the secret step we can take to never be busy again? Create space. Build it in. Make sure you always have it. Space in your day, space in your week, space in your month. Allowing ideas to percolate, relationships to bake, and years to fully blossom into long and happy lives.

Creating space is the secret step to freeing yourself from the oppression of your busy life.

Let's remember the three ways to create space: the 3 Removals.

Remember the dark caped crusaders with menacing masks holding big, sharp scythes? They hack at parts of your life so you're free to do other things. Space comes from this hacking. Space in your life comes from hacking at choice, time, and access.

1. How to make every decision at twice the speed? Remove choice.
2. What's the counterintuitive way to having more time? Remove time.
3. How to add an hour to the day with only one small change? Remove access.

What do we get by creating space? Tim Kreider wrote "The 'Busy' Trap" in *The New York Times*, where he says: "Idleness is not just a vacation, an indulgence or a vice; it is as indispensable to the brain as vitamin D is to the body, and deprived of it we suffer a mental affliction as disfiguring as rickets. The space and quiet that idleness provides is a necessary condition for standing back from life and seeing it whole, for making unexpected connections and waiting for the wild summer lightning strikes of inspiration—it is, paradoxically, necessary to getting any work done."

Maybe it sounds conflicting. On one hand, we're talking about never retiring. On the other, we're talking about creating space to get more done. But let's remember that retiring means stopping *completely*. Creating space means injecting space into your life so you can properly live it. Thoughts process, experiences reflect, and ideas spark. And burn is even sweeter after that.

Remember the Space Scribble.

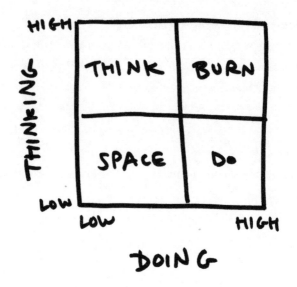

Flip between Burn and Space. Take Thinking breaks. Take Doing breaks. Use the 3 Removals to add to your life. Because life is short. Time is fleeting. And you will never be as young as you are right now.

So develop extra space by Removing Choice, Removing Time, and Removing Access, and nurture that space, that powerful space, so it fills your mind and time and life with contentment, freedom, and happiness.

I want this for you more than anything.

The poem called "Leisure," written by W. H. Davies in 1911, is all about creating space. We have to go back over a hundred years to find the perfect poem talking about how to live a happier life today.

What is this life if, full of care,
We have no time to stand and stare.

No time to stand beneath the boughs,
And stare as long as sheep or cows.

No time to see, when woods we pass,
Where squirrels hide their nuts in grass.

No time to see, in broad daylight,
Streams full of stars, like skies at night.

No time to turn at Beauty's glance,
And watch her feet, how they can dance.

No time to wait till her mouth can
Enrich that smile her eyes began.

A poor life this if, full of care,
We have no time to stand and stare.

BE HAPPY FIRST

DO IT FOR YOU

REMEMBER THE LOTTERY

NEVER RETIRE

OVERVALUE YOU

CREATE SPACE

Have Everything

The privilege of a lifetime is to become who you truly are.

—C. G. JUNG

When I was five years old, my mother always told me that happiness was the key to life. When I went to school, they asked me what I wanted to be when I grew up. I wrote down "happy." They told me I didn't understand the assignment. I told them they didn't understand life.

—ATTRIBUTED TO JOHN LENNON

Nobody can give you wiser advice than yourself.

—MARCUS TULLIUS CICERO

Secret #7

How to Turn Your

Biggest Fear into

Your Biggest Success

1

The childhood trauma that made me quit swimming

D on't be a wimp. Get down here! Get on the slide!"

Wet bathing suit clinging to my sides, I was sitting on top of the curving blue plastic slide, staring down at the bright baby-blue pool and the open arms of the gigantic burly man with a thick black mustache. He taught with my dad and we were at the annual end-of-year school party at the principal's house. Teachers were mingling on the patio near the barbecue and everyone was celebrating the start of summer.

"I'll catch you! Don't be a wimp!"

I was eight years old and couldn't swim but had been playing in the shallow end with my sister Nina all afternoon—watching kids climb to the top of the slide and squeal as they slid down feet first, hands first, face first. Sprinkler water sparkled at the top from a garden hose and slick-greased the slide in the scorching sun. It looked inviting.

Conquerable.

Easy.

I had finally decided to climb my way up and give it a shot. My six-year-old sister swam like a fish and my parents were doggie-paddle pros. I was the family anchor.

"I'll catch you! Don't be a wimp!"

Looking down at the bright baby-blue pool below, I stared into the eyes of the high school math teacher who worked with my dad. Then I took a deep breath and pushed off.

Wind blew into my face, my stomach lurched, and I watched with excitement and then sudden fear as the burly teacher's waiting arms suddenly lifted up into the air as he laughed.

He wasn't going to catch me.

I plunged into the deep end and my vision cut to bright blue horror-film footage. My chest was filling with water and I tried to breathe. Frantically flailing. Hot suffocating pain like I was being smothered by fiery blankets. My eyes lost focus and I was flailing and flailing and flailing until I finally felt big hands grab under my armpits and lift me out.

"See, you can swim!" he screamed. Barbecue smoke, beer bottles, distant laughing. My sister running for my parents. Coughing up water. It felt like glass in my chest.

2

Two barriers we place in front of anything we don't want to do

stopped swimming that day.

Ear infections dotted my childhood, so I was outfitted with neverending sets of tubes. Swimming lessons became skating lessons when I got fancy rubber molded earplugs and a plastic cap for showering.

On summer vacations I would dip into the pool, in the shallow end, or occasionally strap on a life jacket and goggles, clinging onto whatever floating Styrofoam I could find, kicking my way around for a few minutes. At teenage pool parties I didn't bring my bathing suit and made up excuses while sitting on the deck. When friends at college went swimming at the gym I went for a jog on the treadmill instead.

I was afraid of swimming and I became good at avoiding it.

Why didn't I swim?

First, I didn't think I *could* swim. I took a few lessons after the tubes were out. Picture a scared fourteen-year-old who didn't want to get his face wet in a baby pool of five-year-olds picking neon golf balls from the bottom of the pool like circus seals. I quit as soon as I could. I still also had that memory of my dad's pool party. I couldn't breathe, I didn't float, and falling into deep water reminded me of pain.

Second, I didn't *want* to swim! Who cares if I could? I wasn't motivated. What was the big deal? Strapping on a bathing suit meant showing off my spaghetti arms and man boobs. It meant getting cold and wet and chloriney and showering and changing afterward. For what reason? Exercise could be done in other ways. As I got older I told myself the best conversations were at the barbecue or beer cooler. I didn't live near an ocean. So I convinced myself swimming was a waste of time.

What are the two barriers we place in front of our least desirable tasks?

Can't do it!

Don't want to, anyway!

3

The secret scribble to moving from fear to success

et's take a step back.

Swimming was my fear, sure.

But my brain was giving me the same signs we all experience.

In order to do something, we need to think we can do it first and then we need to want to do it second.

Then what happens?

We do it.

We tell ourselves that this is how we get anything done.

Looks like this:

For me, when it came to swimming, I couldn't get past Can Do ("I can't swim") or Want to Do ("I don't want to swim"), so I never got to Do ("I'm going swimming").

I learned the secret to getting those tough things done a few years ago.

Everything changed in a flash when I fell in love with Leslie over a few months. A few dates in and she started telling me over dinner one night how much she loved to swim. "It's my favorite thing to do in the world," she said. "The water just feels like home to me."

"Not me," I said, a bit disappointed. "I don't swim. Not a big fan."

"Well, you'll have to be if you want to come to my cottage. It's on an island in the middle of a lake! We all swim around the island every morning. My ten-year-old cousins. My eighty-year-old grandparents. All of us! You don't have to join, but you'll be the only person sitting on the dock."

I signed up for swimming lessons that night.

Suddenly, without thinking whether I *could do it* or whether I *wanted to do it*, I just *did it*.

I just went online with my credit card and signed up for an Adult Learn-to-Swim class offered by the city at a downtown pool. A few weeks later I was nervously stripping down on a lacquered pine bench in a moldy locker room for my first swimming lesson in twenty years. My heart was thumping. My hands were sweating. I felt like putting my clothes back on and leaving. But somehow I walked out into the pool area and learned one of the most valuable things of my life.

What happened?

Within two minutes I realized I fit in. Who was with me? Recent immigrants from landlocked countries, those with more traumatic childhood experiences than mine, and people from families that didn't have money for swimming lessons when they were kids. I wasn't the worst swimmer in the group for once. We all sucked! Trust formed quickly. Within an hour I was flutter-kicking in the deep end, wearing a life jacket. Within a couple weeks I was jumping in. A month later I was treading water. And by the end of the classes I was doing the front crawl.

I looked like a drowning deer, but my fear was melting.

How did it happen?

This is the secret. This is the big thing I realized. This is the secret you can apply to get anything done that you don't want to do. I promise you it will work.

After my first swimming lesson the idea that I might be able to swim crept into my head. I thought I could do this. And the thrill of flutter-kicking in the deep end gave me inspiration to go back next week and see what else I could do. I wanted to swim now. I love moldy locker rooms. Give me the flutter-board. I was desperate to get back!

My "Do Line" changed to a "Do Circle."

It went from this:

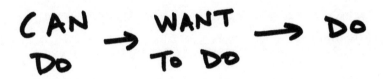

To this:

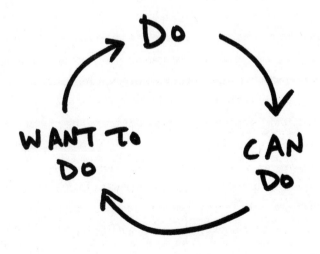

What's the difference? Look at the Do Circle. It's endless. There is no start or finish. It keeps going and going and going. You don't have to end at Do. Do can be a starting point! Do leads to Can Do!

What happened in the pool? I did it . . . so I believed I could do it . . . so I wanted to do it.

Instead of finishing at Do, I started there. And *that* made me think I can do. And *that* made me want to do.

Everything happens backward.

You *start* doing, and confidence and motivation *follow*.

I did it. I went to the pool. I got changed. I wore a life jacket. I flutter-kicked.

So I believed I could do it. This was it! I was in the pool. I wasn't drowning.

So I wanted to do it. I wanted to swim. I wanted to keep going. I'm a swimmer!

The Do Circle completely reverses how most of us operate every day.

How do we operate? Like this:

First, I think I can do it. Then I want to do it. Then I do it.

We think we must have the ability to do something, and then the motivation to do it, before we can successfully do it. Otherwise, we'll fail! The risk of looking stupid sits in front of us and gives us fear. It's the way I thought about swimming for years.

What's wrong with that thinking?

Well, it keeps undesirable tasks undesirable by placing our ability to get them done way down the mine tunnel at the end of the rickety railways of self-confidence (Can Do) and inspiration (Want to Do). What happens? Our most desirable tasks are placed way off in the distance with mental barriers dropped in front of them.

Want to write a book? I'll take a writing course to learn how.

Then I'll find the perfect coffee shop to get inspired. Then I'll write a masterpiece.

NNNNNNN!

Want to write a book? Write one page. Even if it sucks. The fact you did it will convince you that you *can* do it. Then you'll *want* to do it! Why? Because we love doing things that confirm our belief that we're able to do them.

Want to start exercising? I'll save up for a trainer or a gym membership and a set of new shoes. Then I'll make the perfect playlist and find a gym buddy. Then I'll become a gym rat.

NNNNNNN!

Want to start exercising? Run out your door. Just run. It doesn't matter what you're wearing. It doesn't matter how far you go. You could run for two minutes to the end of your street and back. The fact you did it will convince you that you can do it. Then you'll want to do it. Then you'll be a confident and motivated person who buys some running shoes for the next time.

So what big lesson did I learn that day?

I learned it's not easier said than done.

It's easier done than said.

4

How does Jerry Seinfeld use this secret to write comedy?

Jerry Seinfeld is one of the most successful comedians in the world. He has Emmys and Golden Globes, and *Fortune* estimates he earns 32 million dollars a year from *Seinfeld* syndication rights alone. A successfully touring stand-up comic. A *New York Times*–bestselling author. He owns almost fifty Porsches. At one point he was the highest-earning celebrity of the year. But in spite of all these accomplishments, Jerry still needs ways to "trick his brain" into getting stuff done.

Just like you and me.

According to an interview Brad Isaac did with LifeHacker, Brad was a little-known stand-up comic touring the New York City comedy scene in the early 1990s when he bumped into Seinfeld backstage at a show. The TV show *Seinfeld* was new and hadn't become a massive hit yet, so Jerry was touring clubs throughout the city. After his set, Brad saw Jerry backstage and saw a big opportunity to ask him if he had any advice for younger comics.

Jerry Seinfeld then revealed to him a way he writes comedy to make it his favorite task every day.

"He said the way to be a better comic was to create better jokes and the way to create better jokes was to write every day," Brad says. "He revealed a unique calendar system he uses to pressure himself to write . . . He told me to get a big wall calendar that has a whole year on one page and hang it on a prominent wall. The next step was to get a big red Magic Marker. He said for each day that I do my task of writing, I get to put a big red *X* over that day."

Guess what that does? Tricks his brain by giving him the incentive to see the longer and longer chain. Who wouldn't like seeing big red *X*'s marking accomplishments on the wall? Now all you have to do is keep the streak going!

Does this sound familiar?

Jerry Seinfeld gets his "work" done by doing it first. That creates the confidence of being *able* to do it. And then the motivation to "grow the chain" and want to do it each day.

5

It's not easier said than done, it's easier done than said

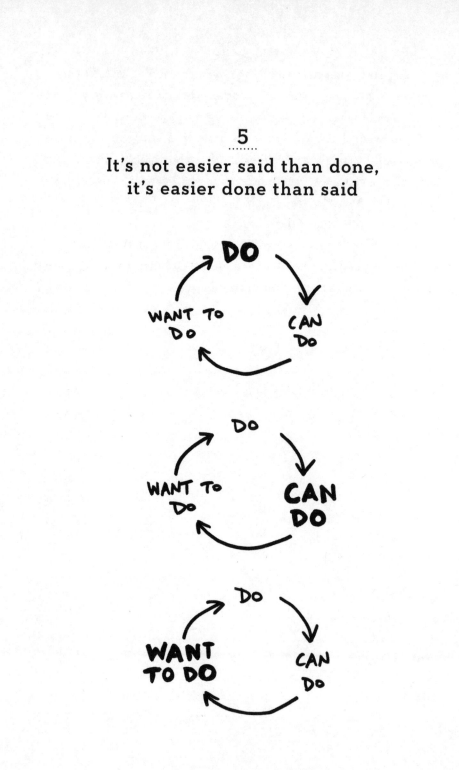

THE HAPPINESS EQUATION

6

A 30-second technique to using this secret in your daily life

How can you *start by doing* in order to get more done?

Here is an anecdote shared by Ramit Sethi, author of the *New York Times* bestseller *I Will Teach You To Be Rich*:

"I was having problems getting myself motivated to go to the gym. Every morning, I'd groggily wake up and say, 'Ugh . . . I know I should get up . . .' and then roll over and go back to sleep. Day after day—even though I genuinely wanted to go to the gym. I finally realized that 'motivation' alone has very little to do with successfully changing behaviors. I started testing different techniques: adding gym to my calendar, sleeping 30 minutes earlier. I would test different approaches for 2 weeks . . . I got mediocre results. But when I sat down to analyze *why* I wasn't going to the gym, I realized: My closet was in another room. That meant I had to walk out in the cold, in my boxer shorts, to the other room, shivering while I put on my clothes. Easier to just stay in bed. Once I realized this, I folded my clothes and shoes the night before. When I woke up the next morning, I would roll over and see my gym clothes sitting on the floor. In fact, I couldn't get up without stepping on them! *The result?* My gym attendance soared by over 300%."

Many people have reported similar results from the Gym Clothes effect. Some even sleep in their gym clothes so they're even "closer to doing" when they wake up. After all, they've already put their clothes on. Might as well go to the gym. My clothes are already on. It would take more work to change into something else.

Spend thirty seconds putting yourself in a situation where it's easier to *do*.

This is me signing up for swimming lessons. Now, if I skipped my first lesson I would have wasted my money. Seinfeld put big red *X*'s on the calendar because he didn't want to leave a day blank. Ramit Sethi put his gym clothes beside his bed. Want to stop eating chips? Hide them in your apartment. Make it easier to not eat chips when you get a craving and are watching TV. Then you won't. And then you'll think you're able to avoid them. Then you'll want to avoid them.

Pulling Do to the front and pushing Can Do and Want to Do into the distance where they don't matter means you'll get more done.

7

What does the greatest physicist of all time say?

First off, who was the greatest physicist of all time?

I say Isaac Newton. My opinion. Up there with Einstein. Why? Well, he discovered gravity, invented calculus, and built the telescope. Not bad! And did he believe in the Do Circle? Absolutely.

He explained it best in his First Law of Physics.

"An object in motion will remain in motion unless acted on by a larger force."

Put it another way: Start doing something? You'll continue.

Why?

Because motivation doesn't cause action.

Action causes motivation.

8

The advertising slogan everyone knows because it follows this secret

Nike said it best.

Just Do It.

They began using that slogan in 1988, and it helped drive market share from 18% to 43% and sales from $877 million to $9.2 billion. Nike struck a nerve! A nerve we all have deep down inside.

Just do it.

Want to feel more confident presenting at work? Don't take public speaking lessons. Don't practice in the mirror. Just do it. Speak at the next team meeting. Just speak. Say one sentence. Then realize you can speak. Then realize you want to speak. Because you know what will happen if you don't? You'll never speak. You'll place speaking in team meetings way down your rickety rails of confidence and desire. You'll take jobs without speaking opportunities. You'll never sign up to present. You'll dissolve into a corporate wallflower.

Don't do *that*.

Just do *it*.

9

The single greatest lesson
we can learn from *Home Alone*

One of my favorite movies as a kid was *Home Alone*. We watched it on TV every Christmas. Kevin gets stranded in his mansion when his family flies to Paris for the Christmas holidays and he's left to discover himself, fight off burglars, and make friends with the scary old man next door.

There's a great scene near the end of the movie when Kevin is talking to that old man. The old man confides that he's fallen out of touch with his son. They're not speaking. He thinks about him every Christmas but can't pick up the phone. Why not? Why can't he do it?

Confidence and motivation. He doesn't think he can do and as a result he doesn't want to do.

I mention this story because in that scene Kevin does a great job explaining what the potential downside is when we confront our fears head-on by just doing them.

KEVIN: I've always been afraid of our basement. It's dark, there's weird stuff down there, and it smells funny, that sort of thing. It's bothered me for years.

OLD MAN: Basements are like that.

KEVIN: Then I made myself go down there to do some laundry and I found out it's not so bad. All this time I've been worrying about it, but if you turn on the lights, it's no big deal.

OLD MAN: What's your point?

KEVIN: My point is you should call your son.

OLD MAN: What if he won't talk to me?

KEVIN: At least you'll know. Then you could stop worrying about it. And you won't have to be afraid anymore.

What's the worst thing that happens if you speak up at the company meeting? You fail miserably. But, as Kevin says, at least you know. Then you don't have to be afraid anymore. And then you can try doing it again or do something else.

What are the chances of failing miserably?

Very low. The greatest leaders just try and try and try. They try. And then they try. And then they try some more. Sure, you will fail at some things. But you'll keep moving. And more often you'll succeed. Little wins turn into confidence and desire to try again, which leads to bigger wins.

You gain momentum.

What did comedian Steven Wright say about building momentum?

"I'm writing a book. I've got the page numbers done."

In that quote, he's describing that invisible butterfly feeling of forward progress we all get in our stomachs when we suddenly just start.

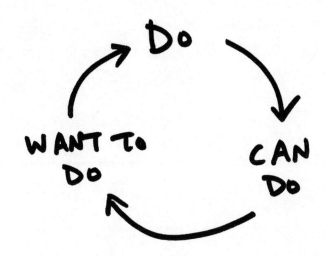

It is easier to act yourself into a new way of thinking than to think yourself into a new way of acting.

Now go forward.

Just do it.

BE HAPPY FIRST
DO IT FOR YOU
REMEMBER THE LOTTERY
NEVER RETIRE
OVERVALUE YOU
CREATE SPACE
JUST DO IT

Secret #8

The Simple
Way to Master
Your Most Important
Relationship

1

"I run a burlesque dancing troupe."

draw muscles in medical textbooks."

"I sell an aspirational online existence."

I stared at the girl with neon-pink hair sitting across the picnic table at the downtown hostel bar, smiled and raised my eyebrows, and took a sip of beer.

I was twenty-nine years old and sitting at a picnic table, a year after a divorce, a year of living alone, a year of therapy, and finally deciding to try online dating. I posted a profile I hoped was authentic. Quirks, weirdness, warts, and all. I spent so long thinking about who I was and what I needed that I had whittled it down to five words: Curious, Creative, Romantic, Optimistic, Ambitious.

I hoped that would all add up to fun and interesting and weird.

As John Lennon said, "It's weird not to be weird."

I wrote about my love of peeling a clementine into one big snaking peel, the dusty warm air before a thunderstorm, and putting one macaroni noodle on each spoke of the fork while eating it. I wrote about how I always peek behind the shower curtain when I'm brushing my teeth to make sure nobody's hiding there. About how I arrange my books in the Dewey Decimal System. About my inability to use a hammer, walk up two flights of stairs without losing my breath, or properly tie my shoelaces. Quirks, weirdness, warts, and all.

Flash-forward a few days and I was suddenly meeting characters from across the city. Interesting people. Out of the woodwork. Where were they all my life? I had coffee with the director of a ballet, went jogging with someone who'd founded a food co-op, and met up with a marketing exec at a coffee-shop lecture about life in the year 3000.

I was having a blast and finally falling in love with myself.

So what's the simple way to master your most important relationship?

Be you.

Be you.

Be you and be cool with it.

There is nobody else you can be better. There is so much of you unique to the world. The deep-down version of you is the best version of all. You are unique and complicated. You are different and dimensional. Those rare thoughts, those flying thoughts, those late-night thoughts, grab on to those and hold them. Those things you think, those things you do, those things you say, those are what slowly helps define who you are to yourself.

Nobody knows every thought in your head. But you do. You hear your thoughts. You should follow them.

Be you.

For you.

Do you know why it's critical to display your true self at work and school and home?

Because:

There is nothing more satisfying than being loved for who you are and nothing more painful than being loved for who you're not but pretending to be.

2
This is the most authentic person of all time

I want to take you all the way back to a peanut farm in Georgia in 1932 where little Roosevelt Grier was born.

Friends called him Rosey and he grew into a 6'5", three-hundred-pound defensive tackle and NFL Pro Bowler. Rosey was a massive guy you did not want to go up against on the football field—he was part of the Fearsome Foursome on the LA Rams. One of the best defensive lines in history.

I love Rosey Grier. But I don't love him for his football career. It's not the sacks, interceptions, or Pro Bowls that are most important. I love Rosey Grier because he was a deeply authentic person. After retiring from the NFL, Rosey let his heart lead him.

He became a bodyguard and ended up subduing the gunman during the Robert Kennedy assassination. He became a recording artist and his song reached #128 on the charts. He became a talk-show host in LA. And my favorite of all? Rosey Grier took up needlepoint. With complete passion. He said it calmed him down, took away his fear of flying, and helped him meet women. In fact, Rosey loved needlepoint so much he wrote a book called *Rosey Grier's Needlepoint for Men.*

Published in 1973 and still for sale today.

Rosey Grier's Needlepoint for Men is trumpeted online with five-star reviews. Rosey let his heart lead him and look where it led!

Now imagine for a minute you were a hulking NFL football player. People staring when you walk into a restaurant. Extra-extra-extra-large shirts. Extra-extra-extra-large jeans. Picture the framed jerseys. Picture the shiny trophies.

Now imagine after you retired, you, a massive NFL football player, went out and published a book about needlepoint. Featuring you needlepointing your own face on the cover!

What would the reactions be? What would *The New York Times Book Review* say? What would your football friends joke about? What questions would you get? Think about that for a second.

Now think how you'd feel if you read this review of your book online:

Most Helpful Customer Reviews

9 of 9 people found the following review helpful

★★★★★ **Lovely book**

By Selma Kahl on December 28, 2011

Amazon Verified Purchase

I bought this for my young neighbor friend that loves the challenge of needlepoint and knitting. At eleven years old, he wants to feel that needlepoint for a young boy is not strange. Needlepoint for men was the perfect gift, His brother is. Into football. And Rosey Grier,s book about needlepoint , brings both those two interests together. It makes both the seven and eleven year old know that it is still manly to want to know and create fine art.

Comment | Was this review helpful to you? [Yes] [No]

3

"Happiness is when what you think, what you say, and what you do are in harmony."

That's the power of being you. That's the feeling you get following your heart.

It's not always comfortable at the beginning, but it's always comfortable at the end.

Marilyn Monroe said, "Imperfection is beauty, madness is genius, and it's better to be absolutely ridiculous than absolutely boring."

Mother Teresa said, "Honesty and transparency make you vulnerable. Be honest and transparent, anyway."

The Mad Hatter in *Alice's Adventures in Wonderland* asked, "Have I gone mad?" and Alice responded, "I'm afraid so. You're entirely bonkers. But let me tell you a secret: All the best people usually are."

Be you.

Be you and be cool with it.

Love your tics and nicks and loves and scratches and fears and passions.

Knowing them leads to living them, and living them leads to loving them.

Your relationship with yourself is the most important relationship in your life.

Settling in to your true, weird, authentic self isn't easy, but it's the most satisfying way to *have everything*.

Let's talk about why.

So many burned-out C-level execs and financial wonders and professional speakers I've spoken to are exhausted coming to work every day . . . pretending to be someone they're not. They think: The pay is so good it's worth taking the role and acting the part. But any misalignment between what you're doing and what you *want* to do allows a dull and invisible unhappiness to fester. Confusion sets into the heart and mind about values. That brain jam—also called *cognitive dissonance*—isn't just exhausting. It's dangerous. Why? **Because your unique sense of self is at risk of being drowned.**

Your unique sense of self that was formed by long summer days and starry twilight dreams and tent conversations and first jobs with great teams—it's at risk of being buried under sandy, windswept layers of cultural expectations. You risk forgetting who you are.

Ralph Waldo Emerson said, "To be yourself in a world that is constantly trying to make you something else is the greatest accomplishment."

But it's not easy.

So why should you aim for it?

Take it from Gandhi. He knew a lot about happiness. He espoused wanting nothing, doing anything, and having everything for himself and his country.

"Happiness is when what you think, what you say, and what you do are in harmony."

Say it again, Gandhi.

"Happiness is when what you think, what you say, and what you do are in harmony."

That's the destination with authenticity. Total alignment of thoughts, words, and actions. Your arms and legs and brain all snapping together with a loud plastic click. Like the cover on the remote control. Snap!

Being you leads to happiness.

But how do we get there?

4

3 simple tests to uncovering
this secret inside you

So let's say you're confident.

Not always. But often. You're not always there but you've gotten there before and you can get there again.

Now you want to listen to yourself a bit. You want to find your authentic passion. You want to be authentic. How do you search your heart and mind to find your authentic self?

After sifting through Harvard visioning exercises and attending endless executive corporate retreats and paging through dusty leadership textbooks I have found what I consider the three best tests to finding and aligning your authentic self. I have shared these tests with countless leaders and use them on myself at least once every year.

Here they are:

1. The Saturday Morning Test
    What do you do on a Saturday morning when you have nothing to do?
    Your authentic self should go toward that . . .
2. The Bench Test
    How do you feel when you put yourself in a new situation?
    Your authentic self will lead you toward that . . .

3. The Five People Test

Who are the five people closest to you in the things you love most?

Your authentic self is an average of those people . . .

The Saturday Morning Test

Let's start with a horrible question.

"What do you want to do when you grow up?"

I worry about that question because it sits invisibly over much of our lives. Professional designations. Business cards. Résumés with job titles and bullet points. These are great things! But the downside to this filtering and organizing is that so many people grow up stuffing their textured, layered, complex selves into narrow buckets that don't allow room for individuality.

Nobody knows what they want to do with their *entire life*. Nobody. Nobody is born with a single unifying sense of purpose that they strive toward forever. Have people at your work ever said "I just backed into this job!" or "I never said I wanted to do this when I was younger. I didn't know it existed!"? My point is it just doesn't happen. Having one giant purpose that you strive toward forever isn't the goal.

What is?

An ikigai.

A current aim.

A reason to get out of bed in the morning.

The Saturday Morning Test helps find an authentic passion and check if you're letting that passion be as big a part of your life as it could be.

The Saturday Morning Test is your answer to one simple question:

WHAT DO YOU DO ON SATURDAY MORNING WHEN YOU HAVE NOTHING TO DO?

Ask yourself that one crucial question, think about it for a second, and answer it out loud. What do you do on Saturday morning when you have nothing to do? Do you go to the gym? Do you record yourself playing guitar? Take whatever answer you have and then wildly brainstorm ways you can pursue opportunities that naturally spew from that passion.

There will be hundreds.

Love going to the gym? Personal training, coaching a baseball team, volunteering for a walking group, running a yoga studio, teaching phys ed, starting a supplements company. And it goes on. Love recording yourself playing guitar? How about teaching guitar online, editing music, learning to DJ, starting up an instrument company? One of the happiest people I've met was a high school music teacher who decided to start importing, selling, and teaching the ukulele.

Your true self will be drawn to these ideas.

They make you richer, stronger, and happier in your work life, too.

Dale Carnegie said, "Are you bored with life? Then throw yourself into some work you believe in with all your heart, live for it, die for it, and you will find happiness that you had thought could never be yours."

The Saturday Morning Test asks you to lean in to your natural passion to enrich your work and personal lives.

The Bench Test

I met Fred Thate in July 1998 in the SHAD program.

Vancouver was our home during this month-long summer camp for teenage nerds as we bounced between astrophysics lectures, particle accelerator field trips, and long conversations on the ocean-side campus of the University of British Columbia.

Geniuses are hard to spot, but Fred was a certified genius in my book—crisp thoughts, sharp observations, a piercingly insightful view of the world. I knew he was going far, but I was eighteen, he was seventeen, and our masking-tape-stuck friendship got tossed on the shelf when we went to different colleges and got immersed in our own lives.

Years later I Googled him and saw he worked as an investment banker in New York City. I cold-called the place and politely asked for Frederic Thate, please. When he answered his desk line, I said "Hey Fred, it's Neil Pasricha," and it was a mini–telephone reunion. I planned a trip down to New York to hang out with him for a weekend.

I spent four years at Queen's, he spent four years at Princeton, and we were eager to hear about each other's experiences. We spent an hour searching for the blue whale in the Museum of Natural History as we caught up.

"So how'd you pick Princeton, anyway?" I started. "I mean, I knew you were smart and all, but why not Harvard or Yale or Cornell or Columbia?"

"Well, I was lucky, I had some options," he humbly mumbled. "I didn't know where to go, so I made a test to figure it out. I called it The Bench Test.

"Basically, I figured I could rent a Jeep for a week for two hundred dollars. And I knew making this decision was worth more than two hundred dollars. So I rented a Jeep and visited Harvard, Yale, Princeton, Brown, Dartmouth, and Columbia. At each campus I walked around until I found a bench near the middle of campus. Then I sat in the bench for an hour and listened. I watched the students and listened to all the conversations around me. I listened to what was important to them, how they talked to each other, what they were excited about."

"How'd you decide to do that?"

"Well," Fred continued, "I figured most of my time over the next four years would be spent doing exactly what I was listening to. Going to classes was twenty or thirty hours a week, tops. The rest is making friends, chatting on the way to class, figuring out plans. Basically, my experience was going to be the sum of all the conversations I had over four years. So I tried to hear those conversations and figure out if they were a good fit for me. I tried listening to my authentic self and letting it lead me toward the right decision."

I was impressed.

I knew hundreds of people who went to university. I knew the majority spent time paging through websites, going on campus tours, and visiting the library stacks—researching for hours the pros and cons from the books. That's what I did.

But The Bench Test was so much simpler than all that. Fred didn't ask anybody where he should go to school, because he knew their opinions were based on their experiences. Not his. He didn't bother with campus tours highlighting famous statues and state-of-the-art treadmills. He didn't sift through campus demographics and SAT score sheets in university guidebooks.

He didn't care.

He just went to campus and sat on a bench.

The Bench Test worked for Fred because **he immersed himself** in the new situation he wanted to test and then patiently observed his authentic reaction to that situation. That's what The Bench Test is about. Really putting yourself into something new for a short time to test it.

Can you use The Bench Test in other places? Absolutely! Just call it The Office Tour Test during your job interview, The Sidewalk Test when you're looking for a home, The Treadmill and Shower Test when you're looking for a gym.

Think about going for an interview at a new company. You're desperate to learn about the company culture and the workplace. Should you ask, "What's the culture like?" No! I get asked that so often in interviews. But that's like reading about school in a book or learning to drive a car in a classroom. You need to get into the office. You need to feel the culture.

How?

The Office Tour Test.

Ask for a five-minute walk around the place after your interview.

You may not be able to sit on a bench, but you'll see everything you need to know.

I'll never forget my first tour of the Walmart Home Office during my job interview.

Sitting on cheap, wobbly, garage-sale chairs in the humming front reception, I watched a motley crew of smiling fiftysomethings, flashy thirty-year-olds, and baby-faced college grads quick-walking in and out of the place. It was like an animated Office Diversity poster. Nobody was dressed up. People were all ages. Nobody was using big words.

The walls were full, too!

I walked past the company mission in block letters: WE SAVE PEOPLE MONEY SO THEY CAN LIVE BETTER. I liked that they knew what they were doing and talked about doing it. There was a flow-chart of the company's history. Rankings of the "Top 5 and Bottom 5 Vendors." And a cutout sign with "Today's Share Price" listed and the sentence "Tomorrow depends on you!"

I walked around with my interviewer Antoinette as she led me down a long hallway and up a flight of stairs. On the way she said hi to every single person by name and they said hi to her by name, too. I felt like we were on a red carpet. "With a thousand people working here, how do you know everyone?" I asked her.

"Easy," she replied. "We have the ten-foot rule. You say hi to everybody within ten feet of you. It's based on asking customers how you can help in a store. Our name badges have our names printed in big letters and we hang them on our shirt collars so they're easy to read. It's like those HELLO MY NAME IS stickers at parties. Except we wear them all the time."

The culture wasn't for everybody.

But I loved it immediately.

The Bench Test is immersing yourself in a new situation and observing your reaction to make sure your decision is aligned with your authentic self.

The Five People Test

"The company is the five people you sit beside."

My leadership professor at Harvard said this all the time. What did he mean? The five people on your team, the five people you eat lunch with every day, the five people telling you all about the company—they are the company. They create and help articulate your view of the company.

"Are your friends making you fat?" asked *The New York Times*, with an article and research studies concluding that even our weight may be based on the weight of our friends. Hang out with fat people? You become fat. What if they hang out with fat people? They become fat. Then you become fat. Sad but true. Some studies have even suggested you're the average of your friends' height and their attractiveness. Makes sense when you see old married couples that look the same. Or people who look like their dogs!

Researchers Nicholas Christakis and James Fowler write in their bestselling book *Connected*: "We discovered that if your friend's friend's friend gained weight, you gained weight. We discovered that if your friend's friend's friend stopped smoking, you stopped smoking. And we discovered that if your friend's friend's friend became happy, you became happy."

Bestselling author James Altucher took the idea even further in the main points of his "The Power of Five" article: "You are the average of the five people around you. . . . You are the average of the five things that inspire you the most. . . . My thoughts are the average of the five things I think about. . . . My body and mind are the average of the five things I 'eat.' . . . I am the average of the five things I do to help people each day."

Remember this: You are the average of the five people around you! You're the average of their intelligence, you're the average of their looks, you're the average of their positivity, you're the average of their creativity, you're the average of their ambition.

So what's The Five People Test?

Take a look at the five people closest to you and remember you're the average of them.

There's you in the middle.

Want to know how positive you are? Average the attitude of the five people you spend time with most.

Want to know how strong a leader you are? Average the leadership qualities of your five closest peers.

Want to know how confident you are? Average the confidence of the five people you hang out with most.

Sure, it's an approximation, but The Five-People Test shows us who we are . . . to ourselves. It's one of the three tests you can use to find your authentic self.

As American philosopher William James said, "Wherever you are it is your own friends who make your world."

5

The 5 greatest regrets of the dying and how to avoid them

Bronnie Ware is an Australian palliative nurse who spent years taking care of the dying in the last three months of their lives. "When questioned about any regrets they had or anything they would do differently," she says, "common themes surfaced again and again."

She eventually put together the five most common regrets from people moments away from their last breath and posted it online. It went viral, and the story was picked up by *The Guardian* and *The Daily Mail*, among others.

So what were the greatest regrets she heard from patient after patient? Didn't make enough money? Didn't work enough hours? Not enough vacations? Not enough homes?

No. You know that by now. The 5 Greatest Regrets of the Dying are:

I wish I'd had the courage to live a life true to myself, not the life others expected of me

I wish I hadn't worked so hard.

I wish I had the courage to express my feelings.

I wish I had stayed in touch with my friends

I wish that I had let myself be happier

Every time I read this list I am stunned into silence for a minute. I think how many of these regrets I would have if I died today. There are always a couple I can work on, and this list serves as inspiration. But one thing I also notice is this entire list relates to authenticity. Directly. It's all about being you.

What happens if you be you and be cool with it? Well, I would argue if you're being yourself, then:

You *do* live a life true to yourself.

You *do* overvalue your time and find a job that fits your life.

You *do* express your feelings.

You *do* keep in touch with your friends.

You *do* let yourself be happier.

Being you removes regrets from your life.

Authenticity removes regrets from your life.

Here are a few additional observations from Nurse Bronnie that were shared in *The Guardian*. Notice how they relate to authenticity:

"I wish I'd had the courage to live a life true to myself, not the life others expected of me—This was the most common regret of all. When people realize that their life is almost over and look back clearly on it, it is easy to see how many dreams have gone unfulfilled. Most people had not honored even a half of their dreams and had to die knowing that it was due to choices they had made, or not made."

"Many people suppressed their feelings in order to keep peace with others. As a result, they settled for a mediocre existence and never became who they were truly capable of becoming. Many developed illnesses relating to the bitterness and resentment they carried as a result."

"I wish that I had let myself be happier—This is a surprisingly common one. Many did not realize until the end that happiness is a choice. They had stayed stuck in old patterns and habits. The so-called 'comfort' of familiarity overflowed into their emotions, as well as their physical lives. Fear of change had them pretending to others, and to their selves, that they were content. When deep within, they longed to laugh properly and have silliness in their life again."

6

"When there are no enemies within, the enemies outside cannot hurt you."

There is nothing as gratifying as living a life where you are you. Because you can't be who you're not.

The Bhagavad Gita, the sacred Hindu text, says it's better to live your own destiny imperfectly than to live an imitation of somebody else's life with perfection. Pretending to be Better You instead of Normal You means spending energy focusing on this person and then acting them into existence. How exhausting! If you were a computer, this would be spending brainpower to flash a beautiful screen saver at everyone walking by. It takes time and energy. And goes against your natural desires and dreams. It's also impossible to thoughtfully do both at the same time. Don't get us started on multitasking, right?

It's hard meeting people willing to share their authentic selves when you first meet them. Chris Rock said, "When you meet somebody for the first time, you're not meeting them. You're meeting their representative!"

But unless that relationship lasts only a few moments, there's so much value in sharing your whole self right away. I say share your deeply authentic self far and wide. Be weird and be random. Be you and be cool with it.

Do you think it's hard to do this? If you do, you're right. It is very hard.

Antoine de Saint-Exupéry says, "How desperately difficult it is to be honest with oneself. It is much easier to be honest with other people. What is true is invisible to the eye. It is only with the heart that one can see clearly."

Chuck Klosterman says, "I honestly believe that people of my generation despise authenticity, mostly because they're all so envious of it."

Herman Hesse writes in *Siddhartha*, "What could I say to you that would be of value, except that perhaps you seek too much, that as a result of your seeking you cannot find."

But if you find it, if you discover and share your authentic self, it has the biggest payoff of all.

Eckhart Tolle says, "Only the truth of who you are, if realized, will set you free."

An ancient African proverb says, "When there are no enemies within, the enemies outside cannot hurt you."

⸎ Shakespeare writes, "This above all: To thine own self be true, And it must follow, as the night the day, Thou canst not then be false to any man."

Remember the Confidence Box. You can't be yourself until you hold a high opinion of yourself and others. Remember the Three Simple Tests: The Saturday Morning Test, The Bench Test, The Five People Test. They will point you the right way.

What happens if you don't share your true self with the world?

Well, then you may never truly know who might love the person you hide.

Be you.

BE HAPPY FIRST

DO IT FOR YOU

REMEMBER THE LOTTERY

NEVER RETIRE

OVERVALUE YOU

CREATE SPACE

JUST DO IT

BE YOU

When I was a kid I always loved albums with a secret track. You know, you played all the way through, you kept the disc spinning, and then five minutes later a song started playing over your speakers. What was this song? What were the lyrics? Why wasn't it in the liner notes?

But there was nothing.

No title. No lyrics. Just music.

To me the secret song always sounded like a reflection of the album but different from the album. Over time, more and more artists started including secret songs at the end of their album. The Beatles. Nirvana. Coldplay.

But I have never read a book with a secret chapter.

This chapter isn't on the Contents page. It's not in the index. It has no page numbers. This chapter is completely off the grid.

And it contains a special secret that's not just about you. It's about your relationship with your partner. That's why I wanted it separate. The rest of the book is just you.

This one?

It's a little different.

The law of being happy together

I have a positive attitude about 80% of the time. Good mood. Happy times. Life feels great. You don't want to see me the other 20%! Sullen, moody, negative. I wish I were positive 100% of the time. But I have never seen anyone there. I'm not saying it's not possible! Just hard. Remember the single biggest reason it's so hard to be happy? And the Culture of More versus the Culture of Enough?

I'm happy I'm happy most of the time. I put a lot into The Big 7 to lift myself into greater positivity.

What about Leslie? She's positive about 80% of the time, too. Enthusiastic and uplifting and happy. Her smile lights up the room. Like me, she's not perfect, and she has off days, too. We all do. But she's one of the happiest people I've met. I love being around her.

What do those two percentages help us with?

It helps us do math!

Yes, I put the exclamation mark there to get you excited about math. I hope it worked. Truth is, the whole world is math. It's the basis of your furniture and car and the way the birds fly and the way the beer pours and the way the stars shine. You don't have to be good at math to love it.

The other good news is you don't need a calculator for this math because there's a table coming and I did all the calculator-punching for you.

So, why are our happy percentages so important?

If I'm happy 80% of the time and Leslie's happy 80% of the time, how often are we in good moods together? 64%. How did we get 64%? Because 80% times 80% is 64%. That's when our good moods overlap. A full two-thirds of the time! We're both smiling and loving and happy and life is funny and moments are precious and everything is in its right place. These are the great days. The great moments. The best side of life.

How often are we in bad moods together? The answer is 4% of the time. Because 20% times 20% is 4%. Those aren't beautiful scenes! I feel bad about them. It's hard giving each other a mood or energy lift if we're both feeling off. Luckily, it doesn't happen too often. Just 4% of the time.

What does this mean?

It means the other 32% of our time one of us is happy and one of us is not. A full third of our time together! A full third of our time together, one person's mood influences the other's. The positive person pulls the negative person up or the negative person pulls the positive person down. Most partners find this number is quite high. You can do the math on yourself to find out yours. Why is this number important?

Because you need to ask yourself an important question right now.

And you need to be honest.

What percent of the time are you happy and what percent of the time is your partner happy?

If you're not in a relationship right now, think about this question with your boss, roommate, or sibling. Whoever you see more than anyone. Whoever has the most opportunity to influence your mood.

You can use this scribble to help:

MY HAPPY PERCENTAGE

MY PARTNER'S HAPPY PERCENTAGE	0%	10%	20%	30%	40%	50%	60%	70%	80%	90%	100%
0%	0%	0%	0%	0%	0%	0%	0%	0%	0%	0%	0%
10%	0%	1%	2%	3%	4%	5%	6%	7%	8%	9%	10%
20%	0%	2%	4%	6%	8%	10%	12%	14%	16%	18%	20%
30%	0%	3%	6%	9%	12%	15%	18%	21%	24%	27%	30%
40%	0%	4%	8%	12%	16%	20%	24%	28%	32%	36%	40%
50%	0%	5%	10%	15%	20%	25%	30%	35%	40%	45%	50%
60%	0%	6%	12%	18%	24%	30%	36%	42%	48%	54%	60%
70%	0%	7%	14%	21%	28%	35%	42%	49%	56%	63%	70%
80%	0%	8%	16%	24%	32%	40%	48%	56%	64%	72%	80%
90%	0%	9%	18%	27%	36%	45%	54%	63%	72%	81%	90%
100%	0%	10%	20%	30%	40%	50%	60%	70%	80%	90%	100%

Take your happy percentage, take your partner's happy percentage, and look at the number in the box where they meet. This is how often you're happy at the same time. Remember or write down this number!

Now, how often are you unhappy at the same time? These are the toughest times, the challenging days, where fights, stress, or friction happen. You can actually just use the scribble from the previous page again. Take your percentage, take their percentage, and look at the number in the box where they meet. This is how often you're both unhappy. Again, write down or remember this number!

Now, once you know how often you're both happy, and how often you're both unhappy, what's left? Well, what's left is how often one of you is happy and one of you isn't. This is how often you influence each other's happiness. You are either pulling your partner up or dragging them down or they're pulling *you* up or dragging *you* down. You can find this percentage using each of your happy percentages. How? That's the second scribble below:

This is the percentage remaining!

MY HAPPY PERCENTAGE

MY PARTNER'S HAPPY PERCENTAGE	0%	10%	20%	30%	40%	50%	60%	70%	80%	90%	100%
0%	0%	10%	20%	30%	40%	50%	60%	70%	80%	90%	100%
10%	10%	18%	26%	34%	42%	50%	58%	66%	74%	82%	90%
20%	20%	26%	32%	38%	44%	50%	56%	62%	68%	74%	80%
30%	30%	34%	38%	42%	46%	50%	54%	58%	62%	66%	70%
40%	40%	42%	44%	46%	48%	50%	52%	54%	56%	58%	60%
50%	50%	50%	50%	50%	50%	50%	50%	50%	50%	50%	50%
60%	60%	58%	56%	54%	52%	50%	48%	46%	44%	42%	40%
70%	70%	66%	62%	58%	54%	50%	46%	42%	38%	34%	30%
80%	80%	74%	68%	62%	56%	50%	44%	38%	32%	26%	20%
90%	90%	82%	74%	66%	58%	50%	42%	34%	26%	18%	10%
100%	100%	90%	80%	70%	60%	50%	40%	30%	20%	10%	0%

For Leslie and me, we're both happy 64% of the time, and both unhappy 4% of the time, so 32% is up for grabs.

Find your own percentage. What do you notice?

The person we're with affects our happiness tremendously. If I'm happy 80% of the time and my partner is happy only 50% of the time, then suddenly 50% of our time is up for grabs. Half of how we feel! We're pulling and dragging each other into good and bad moods. Half the time! And I walked into this feeling great 80% of the time. What an energy drag.

Remember The Five People Test.

You are the average of the five people around you.

But you are an even bigger average of the one person around you most.

You are tremendously influenced (or you spend a lot of energy influencing) the specific mood and energy of your partner.

What's the learning?

It is really important to find a partner who is at your level of happiness. Or higher. The good news is that you can Be Happy First (Secret #1). But it could be exhausting cheering somebody up all the time. So think whether your partner is adding to your happiness or draining it.

Secret #9

The Single Best

Piece of Advice

You'll Ever Take

1

"Ninety-seven percent of lung cancer patients are smokers and ninety-seven percent of smokers never get lung cancer."

Extra Calcium and Vitamin D Aren't Necessary."

The headline caught my eye as I was clicking through the "Most Emailed" section of *The New York Times*. I read how the Institute of Medicine, an independent nonprofit run by US and Canadian governments, had studied more than a thousand publications and come to this conclusion. I suddenly felt better about myself. I wasn't taking any extra calcium or vitamin D. No need to start now.

I then clicked over to the *Toronto Star*'s website and surfed around a bit there.

A headline caught my eye.

"Go on the Offense and Get Your Vitamin D."

Another study, another article, completely opposite advice.

Two of the world's largest newspapers, two big brands, two front-page articles, both giving the exact opposite advice.

What am I supposed to do now?

I suddenly got worried.

What if all advice conflicts?

"Don't take advice."

I remember a CEO telling me this once when I told him some people liked the new corporate meeting and some people didn't. I looked at him. Don't take advice? Really?

"You've done your research, you own the meeting, you don't have to worry what anyone thinks," he said. "You get to decide. And remember that all advice conflicts. You can twist advice any which way to make any point you want. Have you heard that ninety-seven percent of lung cancer patients are smokers and ninety-seven percent of smokers never get lung cancer?"

I stared at him blankly.

I didn't know if that was true, but my brain was lighting up just thinking about it.

He was challenging me.

He always did.

"You make up your own mind. My advice is to become creatively indifferent to all advice. Hear it, but decide what to do yourself." He paused and then said it one more time.

"Don't take advice."

2
....
What can we learn from the most common advice of all?

While clicking around those newspaper websites with opposing headlines, I asked myself, "What advice is most commonly accepted as truth?" Be happy first? Do it for you? Remember the lottery? No. What advice do we all know regardless of our background or experiences?

It suddenly hit me.

Clichés.

Advice that's been said so many times it's become well known to everybody. A rolling stone gathers no moss. A bird in hand is worth two in the bush. Actions speak louder than words. We all know clichés! But what is a cliché, anyway?

Cliché: an expression or idea which has been used and overused because it is or was once considered meaningful.

I also learned that *cliché* comes from the French. In old printing presses, a cliché was a physical metal printing plate that was also called a stereotype. Over time it made sense to cast commonly used phrases in a single slug of metal instead of letter by letter. So a cliché was a collection of words used together often.

Once I learned what a cliché was, I started looking up lists of clichés.

The most timeless advice of all.

I found as many as I could.

And guess what I saw?

Lots of clichés conflict, too!

What's the single biggest problem with all advice you will ever receive?

The fact there is no such thing as rock-solid advice.

There just isn't any.

No advice bird in the bush (what if you're vegetarian?), nothing you can hang your hat on (what if you don't wear hats?), and nothing you can take to the bank (or bank online?).

  – **Advice is never objectively true in all situations.**

How unsettling!

What's the proof?

Defense wins championships	The best defense is a good offense
Birds of a feather flock together	Opposites attract
You're never too old to learn	You can't teach an old dog new tricks
Clothes make the man	You can't judge a book by its cover
Absence makes the heart grow fonder	Out of sight, out of mind
Nothing ventured, nothing gained	Better safe than sorry
You get what you pay for	The best things in life are free

Good things come to those who wait	The early bird gets the worm
The pen is mightier than the sword	Actions speak louder than words

﹀ The proof is that even well-worn clichés look flimsy lined up against their exact opposite.

All advice conflicts!

Have you ever decided what school to go to? Do you notice everyone has a different opinion? Ignore them. Go with The Bench Test. Follow your heart. Have you ever told people what you're naming your baby? Bad idea. Advice comes flying at you. Have you tried asking for advice on what job to do next in your career? Go up, go across, just leave? Everyone says something different. Everyone says go somewhere different and do something different.

Recently, a friend of mine announced she was quitting. Some said, "Great idea, you're free, get out of here!" and others said, "You're an idiot! This is the best place to work."

Remember: Advice reflects the adviser's thoughts, not your thoughts.

Ads tells you one thing, your boss says another, parents tell you one thing, friends say another.

And advice is important for a while.

Watch out for cars. Don't eat worms. Flush the toilet.

But happy people know when it's important to stop taking advice and start listening to yourself.

﹅ **Any cliché, quote, or piece of advice that resonates with you only confirms to your mind something you already know.**

Charles Varlet wrote back in 1872, "When we ask advice we are usually looking for an accomplice."

That's why we like certain advice and don't like other advice. It's the reason people read newspapers that conform to their views as opposed to the ones against them.

So what's the single best piece of advice you'll ever take?

Don't take advice.

The answers are all inside you.

Think deep and decide what's best.

Go forth and be happy.

And don't take advice.

Thank You

Always remember there are only three goals.
To want nothing. That's contentment.
To do anything. That's freedom.
To have everything. That's happiness.
What are the nine secrets to get us there?

BE HAPPY FIRST

DO IT FOR YOU

REMEMBER THE LOTTERY

NEVER RETIRE

OVERVALUE YOU

CREATE SPACE

JUST DO IT

BE YOU

DON'T TAKE ADVICE

Acknowledgements

Thank you.

Life is just a series of conversations, and that was one of the best conversations of my life. We've shared ideas, had lots of laughs, and grown together. I am so grateful to everyone who helped get us to this place.

To all the incredible people at G. P. Putnam's Sons and Penguin Books, we are playing a team game. And you are my team. Special thanks to Ivan Held for your vision for this book and your belief in me. We're on an exciting road.

To my editor, Kerri Kolen, where did you come from? You made me believe in fate. Thank you for your strength, conviction, and passion. You are top class, world class, and all class. I love working with you.

To my agent, Erin Malone, thank you for your fire and energy. We're on such a wild ride together. Thank you for the ticket.

To the teams at Speaker's Spotlight, Washington Speakers Bureau, The Lavin Agency, and Hi-Cue, thank you for spreading happiness around the world.

I am constantly inspired by great writers and artists whose passion broadens me and keeps me pushing. Thank you to Steve Toltz, Mohsin Hamid, David Mitchell, Alice Munro, Charlie Kaufman, Spike Jonze, Tim Ferriss, Nicole Katsuras, Rainn Wilson, Bill Waterson, Stephen Malkmus, Wayne Coyne, and Matt Berninger.

Thank you to the many friends who supported and guided me while writing this book. Special thanks to Brian Shaw, Francesco Cefalu, Scott Broad, Rita Stuart, Gale Blank, Bob Hakeem, Chris West, Plezzie Benitez, Agostino Mazzarelli, Gary Johnston, Mike Jones, and Fred Thate.

To Chad Upton, thank you for your energy.

To Frank Warren, thank you for your wisdom.

To Kevin Groh, thank you for being the ideas man.

Thank you to everyone who gave me permission to use their cartoons, poems, drawings, essays, lyrics, and ideas in this book. Your work inspires me.

Thank you to books for their wisdom and power. Thank you to the invisible worldwide team who creates them for us all—from sunshine to trees to loggers to mills to authors to publishers to printers to drivers to sellers. I love books so much. Thank you for making them.

To Heather Reisman, thank you for your steadfast belief in happiness.

To Dave Cheesewright, so many ideas in this book came from our long conversations. You are the greatest leader I know.

To Amy Einhorn, thank you so much for believing in me. You made me a better writer.

To my growing extended family, I am so grateful for your love and support. Thank you to Bob, Joan, Donna, An, Mark, Mar, and Jenny.

To the world's most passionate teachers, thank you for everything you are doing. I am the son of a teacher and the husband of a teacher and I see how hard you work to change lives. Thank you to the many teachers who helped me along the way, especially Stella Dorsman, Jim Olson, Shera Eales, Chris Howes, John Plinuissen, Ajay Agrawal, Michael Wheeler, and André Perold.

Thank you to luck and chance for great parents, great teachers, and a great country. We are so lucky. I am so lucky.

To my family, you energize, support, and believe in everything I do. I love you Mom, I love you Dad, I love you Nina, Dee, and Lexi.

Thank you to Leslie, my confidant, inspiration, and best friend. All the arguments, ideas, and scribbles in this book came from our endless conversations. You are woven into every page. You are anything. You are everything. You are priceless. I love you.

Finally, thank you to you. Thank you for a great conversation about finding happiness in the middle of this wild and wonderful world. I am so grateful for you, for this, and for everything.

Take care. And talk to you soon.

Index

medical, 120–21
time-sharing, 195–96
Technology and Culture (Jacobs), 77
TED Talks, 171–73
Teresa, Mother, 242
Texas, University of, 21
Texting, blocking access to, 201
Thate, Fred, 248
3 *B*'s of creating space, 154–155
3 *B*'s scribble, 155
Thinking, balance of doing and,
    147–53
Thoughts, 22, 120, 151–52, 203, 238
    of advisers, 267
    alignment of words and actions
        with, 244
    creative, 157–58
    impact of decision making on, 176,
        179
    jumping between, 163
    negative, 7, 74, 90
Three Men in a Boat (Jerome), 12
Three Walks, 20
Tierney, John, 168–69
Time magazine, 12, 108
Time-sharing, 195
Time vs. Effort scribble, 187
Today show, 36, 162
Tohoku University Graduate School
    of Medicine, 102
Tolle, Eckhart, 258
Tonight Show, The (television
    program), 54
Toronto Star, 34, 263
Trauma, childhood, 213–15
Triumph, facing disaster and,
    62–65
20-Minute Replay, 21

Twitter, 14
Type A superachievers, 150

U

Ueshiba, Morihei, 49
Ulrich, Chris, 154
Unplug, 22

V

Vanderbilt University, 200
Vanity Fair magazine, 162
Varlet, Charles, 268
Video Arts (organization), 198
Voicemail, blocking access to, 200
Vonnegut, Kurt, 80–81

W

Waddington's Auctioneers &
    Appraisers, 158
Walks, 20
Walmart, 115, 199
    Home Office, 250–51
Walton, Sam, 16
Want Nothing, 1–92
Ware, Bronnie, 254–56
Watson, James, 110
WebMD, 14
Welch, Jack, 185
Whitman, Walt, 15
Wikipedia, 121
*Willpower: Rediscovering the Greatest
    Human Strength* (Tierney), 168

Credits

Grateful acknowledgment is made for permission to reprint the following material:

Pages 9–10: Quotes from David Cain used with permission.

Page 14: Tweet by Kelly Oxford (@kellyoxford) used with permission.

Page 16: "Attitude" copyright © 1981, 1982 by Charles R. Swindoll, Inc. All rights reserved worldwide. Used by permission.

Page 62: Photo copyright © Couvercelle / TM / DPPI Media

Pages 80–81: "Joe Heller" used by permission of the Trust of Kurt Vonnegut Jr., Donald C. Farber, Trustee.

Page 82: Lyrics from "You Can't Always Get What You Want," by Mick Jagger and Keith Richards. Published by ABKCO Music, Inc. Used by permission. All rights reserved.

Page 99: Martha Sherrill, personal correspondence to Julie Piepenkotter, October 2011. Reprinted with the author's permission.

Pages 106–108: Excerpt and chart from *Purpose and Power in Retirement* copyright © 2007 by Harold Koenig. Used with permission.

Pages 110–112: Permission to use "Never Retire" by William Safire, originally published in *The New York Times*, granted by Helen Safire.

Page 114: Excerpt from *Stumbling on Happiness*, copyright © 2005 by Daniel Gilbert. Used with permission.

Page 158: Quotes from Nicole Katsuras used with permission.

Page 185: Excerpt from "Speed, Simplicity, Self-Confidence: An In-

THE INSTITUTE FOR

GLOBAL
HAPPINESS

The Institute for Global Happiness is dedicated to improving happiness levels inside organizations.

VISIT OUR WEBSITE AND EXPLORE:

FREE TOOLS

The Institute offers free tools to help managers, leaders, and teams assess and address issues around engagement, teamwork, and happiness.

SPEAKING

Neil Pasricha brings his stories and models on managing energy through change and creating lasting happiness to tens of thousands of leaders around the world each year from Harvard Deans to Fortune 500 CEOs to Royal Families in the Middle East.

BOOKS

Neil Pasricha's five bestselling books on mindfulness and happiness have sold over a million copies worldwide. *Download and share sample chapters for free.*

To receive your free *Happiness Equation Key Resources* please visit:

WWW.GLOBALHAPPINESS.ORG